Catching Our Breath

Catching
Our
Breath

Deborah Holmberg-Schwartz

WOMEN'S HEALTH CLINIC

Women's Health Clinic
3rd floor, 419 Graham Ave.
Winnipeg, Manitoba
Canada R3C 0M3

Writer: Deborah Holmberg-Schwartz
Designer: Manuela Dias, eye to eye design
Illustrator: Erica Smith
Printed in Canada by Webcom Ltd.

The production of the first edition of this journal was made possible, in part, by a grant
from Health Promotion Directorate of Health and Welfare Canada. The views expressed
herein are solely those of Women's Health Clinic and do not necessarily represent the
official policy of the Department of National Health and Welfare.

Canadian Cataloguing in Publication Data

Holmberg-Schwartz, Deborah, 1957–

Catching our breath: a journal about change for women who smoke
Rev. ed

Includes bibliographic references.

ISBN 0-9694787-5-5

1. Women – Tobacco use. 2. Tobacco habits – Treatments. Smoking
I. Women's Health Clinic II. Title

HV5746.H66 1996   613.85'082   C96-900647-0

to my mothers
Kathleen Corrie
Frances Meriah Holmberg

Table of Contents

Preface to the Revised Edition

Completing the work on this revision takes me back to when Women's Health Clinic took the leap and hired a smoker—me—to coordinate the "Women's Smoking Project" in 1988. I'm still impressed by the clinic's spunk in hiring a smoker rather than a smoking cessation "professional" and by their commitment to the belief that given real support "ordinary women" will create their own effective ways of healing.

After three months in my new job I did quit smoking using the methods discussed in this journal. But it certainly wasn't easy. I was faced with completing a new project, while at the same time going through the withdrawal and confusion that accompanies quitting smoking. I certainly had never tried to write without smoking. It wasn't long before the stress of trying to work without the "help" of my old friend the cigarette became overwhelming. I developed a serious case of writer's block and considered smoking again "just until the book was written!"

Thank goodness my friend Karen Luks suggested I read Natalie Goldberg's book *Writing Down the Bones*. I believe it was this book that awakened my imagination enough to provide me with the following dream and as a result the confidence to finish the project and become a non-smoker. The dream went something like this: I am sitting in a room with my friends but I cannot speak because my tongue is tied down by many strings criss-crossed over it. I find a pair of scissors and attempt to cut the strings away, but with no luck. Finally, out of desperation, I decide that in order to get rid of the strings, I must cut out my whole tongue. I draw courage to do this by telling myself that I will grow a new tongue. After cutting out my tongue (which was a bloodless procedure in the dream) I have a serious moment of self-doubt. "What if," I ask myself in horror, "tongues don't grow back?" But at that moment I feel the tingling of new growth and within minutes I have a new, pink, healthy tongue. I proudly show it off to my friends, who up until this point had watched me in quiet worry and disbelief. I say to them, "See, I knew I could do it!"

Although there are a few ways to interpret this dream, I believe on one level the dream addressed how I, like so many women, used smoking as a way to express myself and interact with others. Quitting smoking felt as difficult as "growing a new tongue" because I needed to find a new way of expressing myself or forever be tied to the strings of addiction. I share the dream here because I think it speaks to the risk we take and the faith we need to write or to quit smoking or to make any significant change and how ultimately all of these require *belief in oneself.*

Acknowledgments

Even a small book like *Catching Our Breath* is nurtured into existence by many people. First of all, I am most grateful to Women's Health Clinic in Winnipeg for their commitment to the issue of women and smoking and for giving me the opportunity to revise *Catching Our Breath*. I am especially thankful for the trust, patience and good nature of Madeline Boscoe, who coordinated the revision process. Thanks also to the clinic's Catching Our Breath Project staff Mary Sweeney, Clare Thomas and Sharon Spinks who read the draft and provided feedback. Special thanks to Mary Sweeney for her enthusiastic belief in this program and for sharing her resources. Thanks to Glenda Dean at Fort Garry Women's Resource Centre who has been a consistent supporter of *Catching Our Breath* and who read the draft of the revision.

It just so happened that while I was working on this revision I was also facilitating a Catching Our Breath group at the Nelson Women's Centre in Nelson, B.C. The women in the group were tremendously generous in offering their ideas and experiences and providing me with thoughtful feedback, especially about the Smoker's Wheel of Change. My heartfelt thanks to Cheryl Broccolo, Beryl Clayton, Elizabeth Ferguson, Greylin, Antoinette Halberstadt, Suzanne MacKenzie, Marg McGauly, Romy Rudolph and Rose Sauve.

Catching Our Breath groups, in addition to supporting women who want to quit smoking, are also great places to make friends. My own treasured experience of this is with my friend Judie Guignion who continues to enrich my life and inform my work in this area and who gave her time to read this revision and offer valuable suggestions.

Patricia Rawson, a dear friend and also a member of the advisory committee for the first edition of *Catching Our Breath*, read every draft of the revision, offered suggestions, listened patiently to my ideas and typed a significant portion of this book. Big thanks to Patricia for her time and energy, her keen eye, her excellent editing skills and her gift for diplomacy.

Thanks to Erica Smith for her beautiful illustrations in both the first edition and this revised edition and to Manuela Dias for her fresh way of looking at things and her skillful design of the revised edition.

Researcher and writer Lorraine Greaves deserves thanks for making the time to write the introduction to this edition during an especially busy period in her work. As well, Lorraine has demonstrated the spirit of a true adventurer, writing about smoking from a feminist perspective and thereby blazing a trail with her words and ideas for the rest of us. Lorraine's work has provided clarity, insight and encouragement for many of us who are committed to developing a new approach to the serious health issue of women and smoking.

My life partner Ron Schwartz has been an exceptional friend, loving and accepting me through the various stages of my life, including smoker, quitter, relapser and finally former smoker. The constancy of his belief in my abilities continues to astonish and inspire me. My children Candice, Dustin, Sarah and Jacob were immensely patient, rarely getting frustrated when I declined to spend time with them because "I have to finish *Catching Our Breath*!" Thank you my dear family for the tea, back rubs, support and especially for making me laugh.

Finally I would like to thank my friends Gio Guzzi, Karen Luks and K. Louise Schmidt for always encouraging me to develop my ideas and stimulating my thinking with rich conversation and books. My "new" friend, Jan Wright, was a real help to me, candidly sharing her experiences with smoking and quitting, cheering me on and offering suggestions for the book.

In the seven years that have passed between the first and this revised edition of *Catching Our Breath* the whole study of women and smoking has greatly expanded. Now there are several resources and written materials that address this issue. Thanks is owed to all the people who have contributed to our understanding.

My understanding of women's smoking has also grown over the past seven years, thanks to the women I have met while facilitating Catching Our Breath groups. These women have shared brief passages from their journals which appear as the quotes in the margins of this book. I wish I could thank each of you by name.

Introduction to the Revised Edition

It is a pleasure to introduce the second edition of *Catching Our Breath: A Journal about Change for Women Who Smoke*. This inspiring handbook recognizes that quitting smoking is not a singular act, but rather a journey. Sometimes the process itself is as important as the goal.

To truly understand women's smoking it is necessary to ask women what smoking means to them. Women's own interpretations are central to understanding how and why smoking takes root, persists and sustains itself. Such information, while often overlooked by program and policy makers, is crucial to reducing and preventing smoking in girls and women.

Catching Our Breath encourages women smokers themselves to investigate these questions. While difficult and challenging, this task is bound to lead to insights not just about smoking, but about one's life experiences, hopes and strengths.

In talking with many women smokers over the past decade, I have heard many moving stories and insights about the place of smoking in women's lives. The power of these stories has made me realize that smoking can become a crucial aspect of one's life or identity, and that giving it up is clearly a courageous act.

It is also clear that explaining women's smoking cannot be limited to a singular theme. It is not solely a response to advertising campaigns targeting women, nor an offshoot of women's liberation, both common explanations. It is simplistic to assume that women who smoke are pathetically duped by the culture, stupidly anti-health, or servants of tobacco ads. As women in an unequal society, we may be passive or active, or both, from time to time depending on our situations.

Women smokers name many costs, benefits and functions of

smoking. Many of these are contradictory, a fact that does not escape most women smokers. For example, while smoking may offer a sense of control over the world, it also exerts control. While smoking may help cement some social relationships, it may also create distance in others.

Smoking can also function to check emotions, to create an image, or to offer a dependable source of solace. Eventually, smoking becomes part of a woman's identity. Imagining not smoking is increasingly difficult.

Catching Our Breath addresses all of these complex feelings, functions and contradictions. It offers a space to examine these issues on the route to quitting. After this journey, it is hoped that quitting smoking will be no longer a loss, but a gain.

For society and for women, quitting smoking, or better yet, never starting to smoke, is always a gain. Smoking remains the leading cause of death among women in Canada. It threatens to envelop millions of women in many other countries over the next century, as the smoking epidemic reaches into all corners of the globe.

And yet, our cultural and political ambivalence about tobacco and smoking remains a critical problem. It is hard to prevent young girls from taking up smoking in a culture which still glorifies smoking, and in an economy which profits from it. Indeed, a central and worrisome trend in Canada and many other countries is the current increase in smoking among young girls.

A collective will and effort to focus on women's and girls' smoking is required. INWAT, the International Network of Women Against Tobacco, is devoted to reducing or ending women's tobacco use around the globe. As vice-president of INWAT—which has members from all regions of the world—I am concerned about the future of smoking among women of many races, cultures, classes and countries. Unfortunately, the full global dimensions of the women and smoking problem have yet to emerge.

The tobacco industry developed a gender-sensitive approach to women and smoking almost 70 years ago by marketing cigarettes directly to women. It is ironic that health promotion and program and policy development have only recently seen fit to embrace this approach, often after great resistance.

Many different strategies are valuable in reducing smoking. Some are major policy or program initiatives, often designed to limit availability of tobacco or limit opportunities to smoke. These are important, but in the final analysis women who smoke must make an individual decision to quit.

The path to cessation may be long and winding, and may hinge on encouraging women smokers to analyze the place of smoking in their lives. Quitting smoking is not easy, but it can and should be empowering. Catching Our Breath recognizes this by offering respect and encouragement for women's processes of deep self-examination.

Women's smoking is a statement regarding a woman's relationship with her circumstances. Often, it may help women adapt to those circumstances. If it also serves to make women less angry and more compliant, it may also benefit those around them.

Smoking is both symbol and solace, and often comes to assume a place of considerable importance in women's lives. Therefore, if a woman is contemplating quitting, smoking must eventually be replaced. In this sense, smoking is really society's problem.

When a woman lights a cigarette, what is accomplished, or what is helped? Smoking can be a screen for women, mediating between reality and emotions. Each cigarette helps a bit in controlling life and adapting to circumstances. To solve this key health problem, then, a global effort to improve the circumstances of the world's girls and women may be the very best first step.

—Lorraine Greaves, Ph.D.

Lorraine Greaves is the author of Smoke Screen: Women's Smoking and Social Control, *published in 1996 by Fernwood Books (Canada) and Scarlet Press (U.K.).*

Introduction to the First Edition

On behalf of Women's Health Clinic, I am pleased to introduce this journal. We offer it in the belief that through learning more about ourselves, our habits, and the effects of smoking cigarettes we will make healthy choices.

At Women's Health Clinic, we believe in women's right to choose. We believe that the act of choosing is, in itself, empowering. As feminists, we believe that the process of change is as important as the outcome; means and goals must be congruent. Guilt does not create strength. So feeling guilty about smoking will not help us find the strength to quit. We can choose another path.

Reflecting on our values and our goals helps us to choose what's right for us. At Women's Health Clinic, we trust that women know themselves best. The process outlined in this journal is intended to deepen self-knowledge. Women smoke for different reasons; we respect their experience and encourage them to trust their wisdom.

I encourage other women to join with me in "catching our breath," our strength and our health.

We wish to thank the following women for their invaluable help in preparing this journal: Debbie Holmberg-Schwartz, who coordinated the project, co-facilitated the pilot group, and wrote the journal. Debbie, you are the soul and spirit of this project. Laurel Garvie, who supervised the project and provided guidance and support. Jennifer Dundas, who edited the journal and provided clarity and encouragement. Colleen Clark, who co-facilitated the pilot group and shared her ideas and support. Judy Bard and Tamara Wiebe, who typed the manuscript, were ever flexible and gave lots of encouragement.

Members of the advisory committee, who brainstormed ideas about content and direction for the project, provided support and encouragement, read the draft and suggested changes: Verna Big George, Bev Peters, Nori Korsunsky, Patricia Rawson, Edith Kovaks, Laurienne Ring, Diane McGifford, Karen Schmidt, Bev Millan and Mary Sweeney.

Members of the pilot group, who were dedicated and flexible participants, worked with the draft and made suggestions and comments, gave enthusiasm and support and their quotes for use in the text: Marion Anderson, Marilyn Lindsay, Jane Casey, Shirley Nordal, Angie Cooper, Jean Poole, Gail Dunlop, Cindy Roy and Rosie Feschuk.

There are many other women not mentioned here who have shaped this project. Our heartfelt thanks to all of you.

—Rosalyn Howard
Chairperson, Board of Directors, Women's Health Clinic

I have always known
That at last I would
Take this road, but yesterday
I did not know that it would be
today.

—Narihira

About This Journal

Catching Our Breath is written for women who smoke, and who long to be free of the habit. And it is written for women who don't want to quit but are thinking about reducing the amount they smoke. It is also written for women who are simply curious about the place of tobacco in their lives.

The desire to change is a powerful force. It compels us to examine our lives and raises interesting questions. Why did we start to smoke? What purpose does smoking serve? Can we learn to live happily without our cigarettes? Does quitting smoking really matter? Catching Our Breath can help women explore these questions.

There are many reasons why women smoke and why it's hard to quit. The burden of living with poverty, violence, worry and grief can send us rushing out to find some solace. Smoking can feel like a sanctuary in a world unfriendly towards women. Even when our lives are stable and calm, smoking seems to ease the tedious moments and offer a pleasant escape.

For many women who wish to quit, it is a lack of confidence that holds us back. Perhaps we are discouraged by failed attempts to quit smoking in the past, or overwhelmed by the demands in our lives. Maybe we believe we've been smoking too much for too long to quit. *Catching Our Breath* is based on the truth that each of us has the potential to make changes despite the many forces that keep us smoking.

No matter who we are, *we can* unearth the roots of our addiction and cultivate healthier habits. But *Catching Our Breath* isn't about becoming "pure." It's about being honest with ourselves and realistic about what cigarettes can and cannot give us. It's about getting strong and well enough to live a life of our choosing—a life in which we don't need addictions to cope.

Catching Our Breath is based on the belief that every woman's life is precious and therefore worth the time and effort it takes to quit smoking. There are several suggestions in this journal on how we might do this. Take whatever time you need to explore these ideas. Hopefully, the book is written in a way that will help you feel as though you are in a conversation with other women who smoke. It asks you to listen and also to respond to the ideas.

The path of the book starts with a description of a few habits or *practices*. We use this word because it is rich with meaning. A practice is "a custom, a ritual, a predictable act with predictable outcomes or *a way of being.*" Practise also means to do something repeatedly in order to get good at it. You could say that smoking is a practice that we've practised!

The book begins with the idea of practices for a couple of reasons. First, we will use two of the practices—relaxation and writing—to gather our thoughts and respond to the ideas in the book. These practices will help us to "get at" what's behind our smoking. You can think of them in the same way an archaeologist might think of the different tools she uses to uncover a treasure buried deep in the earth. If she only used a shovel, she would miss many small treasures. It's similar when we explore our smoking habit. We don't want to miss discovering something that's keeping us hooked. Relaxation and writing practices are gentle ways of uncovering what can't be found by reading, talking or thinking.

The second reason we start the book with a description of the practices is because all of the practices help build our confidence to make changes. They open us up to the possibility of becoming non-smokers and offer some alternatives to smoking that we can practise while we read the book and learn more about quitting.

Before we move toward understanding our personal addiction to smoking, we will look at the history of tobacco. In Chapter 3 we trace the shift from the traditional use of tobacco in Native culture to addictive use in society and learn who smokes today.

In Chapter 4 we begin the process of understanding our addiction to smoking by reviewing the history of tobacco in our own lives. We explore some of the reasons we were attracted to smoking in the first place. Once we get a sense of how and why we created our relationship with the cigarette, we can start to think about changing it. In Chapter 6 we discuss change: how we've dealt with change in the past, some common stages we go through as we make changes and a suggestion for a new way to prepare to quit smoking, called the *Smoker's Wheel of Change*.

Each following chapter discusses the ways we use smoking in our lives now and suggests alternatives to bring us closer to stopping smoking. The last three chapters are more specific about what it means to let go of our cigarettes, how we quit, and how we stay off cigarettes. Some of the suggestions are ideas from popular smoking cessation programs. Others are unique. Each chapter ends with a relaxation exercise, followed by one or two journal questions.

You can work with this journal intensively over a week, or slowly for many weeks. It's entirely up to you to determine the pace that feels right. It may take some time to get into the habit of using a journal. One way to help this process is to leave it in sight as much as possible. You may want to carry it around with you.

If some of the ideas feel new or strange to you, try not to reject them immediately. It could be that you need time to think about them. It's important to keep an open mind and to ask that part of you that might be saying "Oh this won't work!" to be silent. Developing new habits takes time and patience. It helps to maintain a sense of humour and to be gentle with yourself. Remember, you can always adapt the ideas so they feel more like your own.

And the ideas don't just apply to quitting smoking. They are more than techniques for stopping a troublesome habit. No matter what our decision is about giving up cigarettes, we could all benefit from practices (such as writing and relaxation methods) which help us deal with stress, increase our self-awareness, honour our bodies and invite more peace and joy into our lives.

But most important, the suggestions in this journal are guided by the belief that *every woman is the expert on her own life.* Just as each woman has her own reasons for smoking, each—in her own time—will have her own ways of quitting and reasons for staying smoke-free. The ideas in this journal are intended to act as supportive and inspiring companions, encouraging women to believe in our ability to change and affirming our unique ways. Our desire to change can transform into action. Good luck!

SUPPORT

Getting support is one of the most important factors in quitting smoking and staying off cigarettes. Whether we like it or not, the people in our lives have a powerful influence on who we are and the choices we make.

Take for example the experience of learning to smoke. We were probably in the company of at least one friend when we had our first cigarette (more on this in Chapter 4). And the behaviour was modelled for us by friends or family members for several years before our first attempt at smoking. If we lived in a smoky environment, our bodies were learning to deal with cigarette smoke, slowly growing accustomed to its effects.

We were shown how to smoke by watching others. We were offered reasons to smoke by the tobacco advertisers and the media (more on this in Chapter 3). We learned when and where to smoke by listening to the reasons of others or by watching them. In other words, we were very supported in starting to smoke.

If you don't believe you were influenced by society to smoke, try to imagine how you would have, as a young teen, thought of taking up this habit all on your own. No advertising, no friends or family smoking, no talk or images of smoking in the media—just packs of cigarettes at the store waiting

"My family has been great. I was worried they wouldn't care after a few days. But every week they surprised me with a little gift."

to be bought. Would you have purchased them and persisted in smoking all by yourself?

Just as it would have been extremely foreign to be a young smoker in a world where no one smoked, it's just as tough to quit without the support of others. It's tougher still if everyone in your life smokes.

It's tremendously important to seek out friends and allies who will encourage the part of us that wants to make changes. Speaking with others about their experiences of smoking and quitting can normalize what we are experiencing. We can gather strength from their successes and learn from their mistakes. "Never-smokers" can show us that it is possible to be an interesting person and to live without ever wanting or missing cigarettes. By watching them, we can pick up ideas about what a person can do instead of smoking.

The people we choose to approach for support must believe in our ability to make changes and take a non-blaming approach in helping us. In fact, no support is better than "help" from a critical, moralizing or opinionated person—relatives can be the worst. Studies have shown that women tend to be more supported by female friends than they do by their male partners. The opposite is true for men trying to quit. They report receiving a lot of support from female partners and not as much from male friends. Women's socialization has taught us to be skillful at offering practical alternatives, such as back rubs, and tolerating the mood swings of others. Society's expectations discourage us from showing so-called negative emotions and putting our needs first. These differences could account for why men generally say they find quitting not so hard while women frequently say they feel thwarted in their efforts.

Even if you are fortunate enough to have a partner in your life who is great at supporting you to make changes, it's still worth clarifying what kind of

> "I've tried quitting lots of times and it was definitely easier this time in a support group. I'd recommend it to any woman."

> "I hate it when I'm not acting that great and someone says, 'Oh, I guess you're cranky because of quitting.' I think, 'Whatever, just leave me alone'. I don't want a spotlight on me because I'm quitting smoking. I was moody lots of times, even when I was a smoker."

help you want to quit smoking. You don't need the stress of arguing about this while you are in the midst of withdrawing. Sometimes our partners are so happy at the thought of us quitting smoking that we can't bear to tell them that we've relapsed or changed our minds. It's important to be upfront that this is your change and that you need to do it your way—even if that means risking your partner's or friend's disapproval.

Take the time to think about what support means to you. How do you want to be supported as you begin to make the change from smoker to non-smoker? If you don't want to tell anyone about your plans to make changes or about using this journal, that's fine. But if you take this route you have to be especially careful to take care of yourself and to avoid difficult situations. Don't underestimate the power of your environment to undermine your good intentions.

"Support, to me, means someone who will listen. I don't want any advice."

IF YOU WANT TO WORK WITH OTHERS

There are three ways you can use this journal. You can read it on your own (following the exercises at your own pace), work with a partner, or work with the support of a group. A facilitators' manual has been produced to guide you through working with a group and is available through Women's Health Clinic. (The address and phone number are printed at the back of this journal.) The manual includes suggestions on how to find women to join a smoking cessation group and offers ideas and information on how to run it. Catching Our Breath support groups have been facilitated in many provinces in Canada since 1989. To find out if the Catching Our Breath program is offered where you live, contact Women's Health Clinic.

Working with a Partner

If you decide to work with a friend, it's important to choose someone with whom you can keep in contact easily. It will be important that you can call one another often and meet in person once a week. Your partner should have ideas similar to your own about smoking and quitting. For example, if she feels quitting is just a matter of "willpower" and you believe there are many other reasons why women don't quit, you could have trouble supporting each other. Your partner should also be a smoker, although it's possible to work with a woman who has already quit smoking.

Another block to working well together may occur if your buddy has a very different lifestyle from yours. If you are on social assistance, struggling to raise children on your own, and your partner is single and working full time outside of her home, you will need to acknowledge and bridge your differet experiences with quitting. Support is the most important reason to work with another woman. The more you can relate to each other, the more likely it is that you will be able to support each other.

When you choose a partner, you should meet before you begin working with the journal. At the meeting, take time to talk about the following:

1   What are my goals?

Do I really want to quit smoking or do I want to just begin to think about quitting? It's okay to not commit yourself to quitting. Let each other know what your goals are, so that you don't impose false expectations on each other.

2   How do I want to be supported?

Some women will just want to be heard as they go through the quitting process. Other women would prefer to have a back rub and a cup of tea rather

> "I asked my neighbour if she'd try quitting with me, since it's usually us two having coffee and smoking together. And she said yes. It's going really well so far. The hardest part has been convincing our kids that we are having a 'support group meeting' when we are at the kitchen table reading the journal."

than talk. State how you think you would like to receive support. Don't worry if things change. You may be surprised at how much you need to talk, even though you never thought of yourself as a talker in the past.

3   What are my fears?

Speak as honestly as you can about your fears about working with a partner. Opening up to another person can be frightening at first. Talking about our fears is the first and most important step in making ourselves feel safe. Failure is a big fear for lots of women. Some women find it helpful to write down their fears along with suggestions for what to do about them.

4   What kind of support can I offer my partner?

It's good to make a short list of ways you can support your partner. Writing out a list can clarify and affirm the different ways you and your partner provide support.

5   What if I need to change the partnership?

You may find that you can no longer continue working together. It will be important to let each other know right from the start that it's okay to end the partnership. Sometimes we find out we're just not ready to work with the journal or that we prefer to work alone. Decide at the start not to make the other person feel bad or guilty for ending the partnership.

6   When and where will we meet?

To avoid confusion and to establish consistency, you will need to decide on a regular meeting time and place. You may want to rotate homes or you may find a separate place to meet. Decide whether or not it will be okay to have children present, if you need a quiet place, etc. Also decide how long your meeting will be. It's very important to make your meeting times as pleasant as possible. You can do this by making sure you have a clear place to work (even if it is just the size of your kitchen table) and a few snacks to share. Some of the exercises require music, so you will need to have a cassette player or stereo nearby.

7   How many pages or sections of the journal will we cover each week?

Decide how quickly or slowly you want to cover the material in the journal. It's okay if you change your minds about this later on. The important part is to make sure that there isn't a conflict between your expectations. If one of you wants to move very slowly and one of you wants to move rapidly through the journal, you could be setting yourselves up for disappointment. It's impossible to decide how everything will flow before you actually start using the journal. Allow yourselves the time and flexibility to change things if they don't work as planned. Keep your sense of humour, and remember that you can improvise.

The Practices

Sometimes our addiction to smoking can feel so complicated and powerful that we think it will require a very sophisticated and mysterious means to break free of it. But there is no fast and fancy way to quit smoking or make other changes. Lasting change requires focused attention, real effort, hard work and patience. Successful quitters use ordinary and simple ways to slowly overcome their addiction.

Women in Catching Our Breath groups have found the following practices helpful. We review each of these practices during the first session of the program. This gives everyone a chance to get comfortable with the different ways we will explore the subject of smoking. Even if we haven't made a decision to quit smoking, practising alternatives to smoking is still very helpful. For example, learning new ways to relax gives us more options during those times when we simply can't smoke—like at the dentist's office! And it is much easier to give up a habit like smoking if we have a better habit to replace it with.

Remember that it takes several weeks (at least) to establish a new habit. Learning some alternatives to smoking now, in preparation for quitting, will help us avoid the stress of learning a new habit at the same time we are experiencing the discomfort of giving up smoking.

Some of the ideas will be more appealing than others. It's fine to favour one method over another. What's most important is that we make the time to "practise these practices"!

WRITING

Each chapter in the journal ends with one or two questions, which prompt us to explore some of our thoughts about smoking in writing. Writing or "journalling" connects us with a rich source of self-knowledge. When we take the time to write down our thoughts we move beyond the surface "chatter" to a deeper level of ourselves. It is here that we can often describe feelings and ideas in fresh and clear ways that previously seemed beyond words.

Writing also enhances our self-esteem. As we take the time to reflect on our own ideas and feelings in writing, we send a powerful message to our inner selves. We say, "I care enough about myself to listen to myself." If we want to make changes we need to know and understand who we are now.

Because "journalling" is a unique form of communication it can provide unique insights into our lives. These insights can help us prepare to quit smoking and provide encouragement to stay off cigarettes. For example, the discomfort of change can easily send us retreating to predictable habits. Writing is a way to acknowledge these difficulties, sort through our mixed feelings and find out what we really need and want. It helps keep us awake and on track.

Unfortunately, most of us approach writing with fear and resistance. Our school system is largely responsible for this, since it was within this system that we first experienced feelings of shame and inadequacy over our writing. It could be that we didn't learn to spell or to form sentences to the satisfaction of our teachers. Many of us were heavily criticized and compared to others. We may have been forced to write in a language other than our own. Whatever the reasons, almost all of us have internalized the notions "I can't write," or "I hate writing!" (Internalize means we bring a thought, belief or value about something or somebody into ourselves and make it our own.)

But journal writing is not like the writing done for work or school assignments. Journal entries unfold like conversations, with ourselves. It doesn't matter if we can't spell or form complete sentences. Do not be concerned with punctuation or sentence structure. It is the process of writing that helps us. The writing needs to make sense only to you.

> "I do find journalling helpful. It helps clarify thoughts and feelings and to express myself. I often discover things about myself, which is exciting because it provides understanding."

> "Sometimes, even when I'm sitting there thinking about how much I want to quit, I look down and I have a cigarette in my hand. I just don't get how automatic smoking is. It just seems like my brain is programmed to keep smoking. Writing in my journal is helping me break down my actions into smaller pieces, so I'm starting to see how one thought leads to another. I feel like I'm getting back some control."

Suggestions for Awakening the Writer Within

1 Blank pages are provided in this journal for you to write on, but you may feel more comfortable purchasing a different notebook or journal. If you do, buy a notebook in a convenient size with ruled or blank pages. Make sure the pages are bound so they don't fall out or get mixed up.

2 Buy a special pen(s). You may want to choose a few different ink colours. Consider buying some felt markers or crayons as well.

> "It seemed every time I tried to quit smoking I was overcome by feelings of fear. I hated those feelings so much that I would just go back to smoking. It wasn't until I did the writing exercise about how I first started smoking that I realized that I started smoking after I had been raped. I was amazed to see how I used smoking to deal with the fear of something terrible that happened a long time ago. I never had thought about that before."

3   Choose a time and a place where you will be uninterrupted for at least 20 minutes. If you do the relaxation exercise before writing, you will need about 30 minutes of private time.

4   Write only when you want. Don't place unrealistic expectations on yourself. Writing for a period of 30 minutes once a week is plenty.

5   Try to write as honestly as possible. You don't need to share what you have written.

6   Date each journal entry.

7   If you decide to share what you have written, make sure you do so with someone who won't criticize your writing. It is important that you write for your own approval only.

8   Explore writing or drawing with your opposite hand. Although this may feel strange at first, you might be surprised by what it reveals.

9   Draw, colour or sketch in your journal. Many ideas are expressed better with images than with words.

10 If you are worried about someone reading your journal, find a place to hide it. One woman solved this problem by hiding it in her washing machine. This was the one place in her home that she was sure no one else would ever go near!

RELAXATION

> "Relaxation—with music—is a much-needed experience for most, I'm sure. You can feel the tension drain and for myself this is a spiritual experience."

Each of the writing exercises in this journal begins with a relaxation exercise. There are two reasons why relaxation is one of the essential practices of *Catching Our Breath*. First of all, taking a few minutes to slow down and blow off some of the demands of the day makes it easier to shift into writing. But more importantly, our ability to relax has an enormous effect on our health and our ability to quit smoking and avoid relapse. Taking the time to create moments of calm for our mind and body greatly increases our chance of success.

Relaxing is a learned skill. It requires practice. When we relax, we are better able to get in touch with our thoughts, feelings and needs—and less likely to be overwhelmed by strong emotions such as anger. This might seem contrary to what you have been taught. You may think that you need to "tighten up" and "get busy" in order to solve a problem. In fact, you are more likely to do what's best if you loosen up, slow down and act from a place of calm.

In a relaxed state our heart rate and blood pressure are lowered, and even our body temperature changes. These are amazing facts, considering that up until the last 30 years scientists and doctors believed we had absolutely no control over these basic body functions! Many of us still doubt our ability to cope with stress or change how our bodies work without the help of drugs (including nicotine).

There are some interesting research studies that show that people can use relaxation methods to "train our brains" to produce certain brain wave patterns called alpha waves and theta waves. When our brains are making these waves we feel quiet, happy and alert but also pleasantly detached from our surroundings (Murphy 1992).

As smokers, we have come to associate these same feelings with lighting up a cigarette. And of course the tobacco industry has been busy convincing us that cigarettes are the ultimate relaxation aids. It's true that sometimes when we smoke we do feel more relaxed. This is partly because nicotine triggers the body to release its own natural feel-good hormones called B-endorphins. It's also likely that we have taught ourselves to use the idea of smoking as a mental prompt to shift into the alpha brain wave pattern.

The reality is that smoking increases both our blood pressure and our heart rate—the opposite of

"It took me a long time to get into the relaxation exercise. I'm such a speedy person, sitting still seemed like a big waste of time. But now I love it. It makes me feel like I've had a bath from the inside out."

what we want to happen when we relax. The positive feelings we get when we smoke, including the sense of well-being from our endorphins, can be found in healthy ways. With practice we can learn to relax without our cigarettes.

Conscious Breathing

Relaxing begins with breathing fully and deeply. Our breath has been described as "our first food." It nourishes and supports us. It is with us from our birth to our death. More than anything else, our breath can soothe, relax, heal and energize us. It is our true friend.

As strange as it may sound, most of us don't know how to breathe. We often hold our breath, or breathe using only part of our lungs. Paying attention to our breathing and changing how we breathe can be described as "conscious breathing." *Conscious breathing is probably the most important practice in quitting smoking.*

Ironically, smoking is a misguided effort at conscious breathing. Lighting up a cigarette might be the only time in a day that we stop to "catch our breath." We incorrectly attribute the benefits of taking those long deep breaths to smoking. We have come to believe that smoking is the one constant, dependable companion in a life full of changes and disappointments. But breathing is the true constant. When we quit smoking it's important not to also quit the wonderful habit of taking time to turn inward and focus on breathing.

Practise conscious breathing many times each day, in between the times you smoke. This will help establish a new habit and make quitting easier. You can use everyday sounds in your environment to remind you to breathe. The phone ringing, the baby crying, or the slamming of a door can all be

> "I had no idea how helpful something as simple as breathing can be. I've even taught my kids to do it. They say, 'Breathe, Mommy, breathe.'"

transformed into cues to breathe deeply. Author and meditation teacher Jon Kabat-Zinn (1990) says:

> When we are mindful of our breathing, it helps us to calm the body and the mind. Then we are able to be aware of our thoughts and feelings with a greater degree of calmness and with a more discerning eye. We are able to see things more clearly and with a larger perspective, all because we are a little more awake, a little more aware. And with this awareness comes a feeling of having more room to move, of having more options, of being free to choose effective and appropriate responses in stressful situations rather than losing our equilibrium and sense of self as a result of feeling overwhelmed, thrown off balance by our own knee-jerk reaction.

"Sometimes I'm just one deep breath away from goin' nuts!"

Peace activist and Buddhist monk Thich Nhat Hanh (pronounced Tik Not Hon) has helped thousands of people coping with hunger, torture, war and poverty to use breathing as a meditation technique and path to peace. He says:

> As you breathe in, you say to yourself, 'Breathing in I know that I am breathing in.' And as you breathe out, say, 'Breathing out, I know that I am breathing out.' Just that. . . . You don't even need to recite the whole sentence; you can use just two words: In and Out. . . . As you practice your breath will become peaceful and gentle, and your mind and body will also become peaceful and gentle. (1991)

The wonderful thing about conscious breathing is that it is available to everyone—including the single mom coping with a sick child, the exhausted worker dealing with a nasty boss and the stressed-out student. Conscious breathing is a simple way of nurturing ourselves.

Visualization

Visualization is an expansion of the relaxed state. When we visualize we use our imaginations to create certain scenes or images. For example, you might imagine that you are at the ocean or floating on a cloud. Daydreaming is actually a form of visualization. If you daydreamed as a child, you can certainly relax and visualize as an adult.

"I had no idea what a good imagination I have. Visualizing is fun!"

The images in our visualizations can help us deepen our relaxation, bolster our confidence to quit smoking and ease the discomfort of withdrawal symptoms. If you want to transform a fear or a worry you could visualize it rising like a bubble and bursting, or you could picture yourself handling a difficult situation confidently and calmly, without smoking. If you want to speed up your body's recovery process, you might try imagining your lungs becoming pinker, cleaner and more open.

Visualization can help us achieve many of our personal goals. Athletes, actors and many ordinary people have used visualization techniques to win races, overcome anxieties and phobias, create a piece of art or make a dress. Everything we make or do begins first as an idea in our imaginations. Becoming a non-smoker is no different.

Some smokers use visualization to remember themselves as they were before they started to smoke. These memories of ourselves as non-smokers can inspire us to create a picture of who we want to become. Other women repeat important phrases such as "I am free of my addiction" while picturing themselves jogging or swimming. If this seems impossible, visualize the times when you don't smoke. No one smokes every minute of the day. Remember the times in between cigarettes. These images are extremely potent because they are positive experiences of not smoking. They help us form an identity as non-smokers and help us reclaim the power to feel good—a power that the cigarette has had.

In fact, images are so effective in influencing our behaviours that the tobacco industry uses images in advertisements to manipulate reality. These images connect healthy, positive activities such as windsurfing or mountain climbing with smoking. The tobacco industry is trying to get us to turn to cigarettes to quench our thirst for fun, adventure or peace of mind. It wants us to imagine ourselves happier, healthier and more fulfilled as smokers.

A list of further reading on relaxation and visualization is included at the end of the journal.

"When I'm just getting into my relaxation exercise I'm sure I won't be able to come up with any images, but before I know it one or two interesting little scenes float by in my head."

Basic Relaxation Exercise

The following relaxation exercise takes about 10 to 15 minutes to complete. You may want to play soothing instrumental music in the background. Some women find it useful to tape the relaxation exercise and play it before the writing exercises. If you don't like the idea of hearing your own voice telling you to relax, you might ask a friend (make sure you like the sound of her voice) to tape the exercise. Take the time to move through the exercise slowly, pausing after each sentence. It's worth trying a few versions to create one that you find soothing.

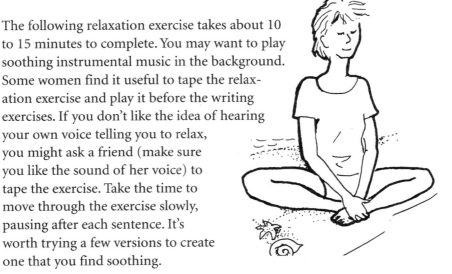

Sit or lie in a comfortable position. Close your eyes and bring your attention to your breathing.

Notice if your breathing is fast or slow, deep or shallow.

Inhale deeply a few times, letting your breath out slowly. Now, just let your breath find its own natural rhythm.

Bring your attention to your body; adjust your position if you need to; scratch or stretch; do whatever you need to feel comfortable.

Take another couple of deep breaths; notice if there are any sore or tense spots in your body.

With each breath in, draw in calm, relaxing energy. With each breath out, let go of tension.

Become aware of your breath moving in and out of your lungs. Feel your chest rise and fall. Be aware of the wonderful work your lungs do to nourish your body with each breath. Know that your lungs' only need is clean air. Give thanks to your lungs.

Breathe deeply now and scan your body. Become aware of your muscles, your bones. Let your breath soothe and relax your body. Allow your body to become open and relaxed from the top of your head to the tips of your toes.

Now bring your attention to the chatter in your head; notice what thoughts are clamouring for your attention.

Imagine that as you breathe you blow away any unnecessary thoughts. If you have some important concerns on your mind, imagine putting them in beautiful boxes and placing them safely away on a shelf, where you can pick them up later.

Take the time now to let go of anything that keeps you from feeling calm and relaxed.

LONG PAUSE

Now picture yourself on the warm, sandy shore of a beautiful ocean. Feel the sun streaming down on your body, feel the wind gently blowing; hear the sound of the waves. With each wave allow yourself to become more and more relaxed.

Stay in this place for a while. Know that you are completely safe and comfortable here. Experience the peacefulness of this place. (If this isn't the kind of place that makes you feel calm, create a different image.)

LONG PAUSE

Remember this place and this feeling. Know that you can return to it whenever you need or want to.

Take a couple of deep breaths, allowing yourself to drift back to this room.

Feel the chair or floor beneath you; notice the sounds in this room.

Breathe deeply, slowly allowing yourself to return to this room, this place.

When you are ready (take your time) you can return completely alert, refreshed and relaxed. When you are ready open your eyes and stretch your body.

If you fall asleep during the exercise, you probably needed the sleep. You can help yourself stay awake by doing the exercise during the times of the day when you feel most energetic. You can also try sitting up instead of lying down. With practice the exercise will relax you, instead of putting you to sleep.

On the other hand, if you feel overly energetic after the exercise you can try stretching your body, shaking your hands, running them under cold water or placing them on the floor for a while. Imagine that you let some of this energy seep down into the earth.

If after several attempts the exercise doesn't seem to be working at all, take a break from it for a few days. Learning to relax is a very individual process that requires patience and a lot of practice. In time you will find the method that works for you.

AFFIRMATIONS

"Affirmations are an excellent source of strength."

Affirmations are positive statements. We work with affirmations in the journal because they are powerful tools, useful in changing limiting or negative views about ourselves. For example, as children, many of us may have been told by our parents or teachers that we were stupid or slow, stubborn or bad. Since we were dependent upon adults for our survival, their words and actions held a great deal of power. We believed what they told us was true—no matter how cruel or destructive.

We carry these toxic beliefs into our adult years, damaging our self-esteem and sapping our confidence. Over time we come to think of these nasty little ideas as truths. We need to rethink these ideas if we want to change, because change requires confidence and courage. If we believe we fail at most things, or lack self-discipline, we rob ourselves of the chance to be successful at quitting smoking.

"I really wish I would have heard these positive things when I was a kid. But I know it's never too late to feel good about myself. I'm starting now."

One way to counteract powerful negative beliefs is to create positive statements to challenge them. If you live with the belief that you cannot speak in groups, you might want to create an affirmation that counters that belief. You might want to practise saying, "I feel confident speaking in groups" or "I am a clear speaker" or simply "I am free to speak."

Affirmations are not magical or mystical. They are simply positive statements that help us build a more accurate self-concept. Affirmations convey the compassionate and encouraging messages that loving parents spontaneously give their children. If we didn't receive this information as children, there's no need to continue to deprive ourselves of it. We can give ourselves what we need to hear now! Affirmations work best if we repeat them (wholeheartedly) many times each day.

You may find this process difficult at first. It's normal to feel embarrassed and even ashamed of your new affirmations. Try not to let these feelings discourage you. If you find yourself doubting this process altogether, remind yourself that the critical ideas you hold to be true about yourself are just someone else's opinions. They are not absolute truths, and you were not born thinking them. You have the power to release these burdensome beliefs. Be patient with yourself and practise!

"I'm sure if I can build my confidence, I'll definitely quit smoking. The affirmations are helping me."

How to Create Your Own Affirmations

1   Affirmations include positive statements about yourself that you already believe to be true as well as positive statements that you don't accept as truths.

Create an affirmation that challenges your idea of who you think you are. For example, it might be easy for you to say, "I am a good cook."

Although it's pleasant to remind yourself of this, it's probably not necessary to spend a great deal of time repeating it. You already accept it. If it is difficult to say, "I am an intelligent woman," then that's the affirmation to work with for a while. Try writing out a few that touch on areas where you feel vulnerable.

2   State your affirmation positively and in the present tense. For example, say "I am strong" rather than "I am not weak" and "I am lovable" rather than "I will be lovable."

3   Say your affirmation out loud and to yourself many times a day. It is also very effective if you

look in your mirror and say it, write it in your journal several times and place written affirmations around your home. It feels wonderful to greet yourself each morning with an affirmation. A powerful one is "Today, I will be true to myself."

4 Try not to skip from one affirmation to another. Give yourself time, a few days at least, to absorb one before moving on to another. Some suggest working with each affirmation for a month.

5 Make sure your affirmation is your own idea and not someone else's idea of what you need. Only you know what you need to affirm about yourself!

6 A good affirmation to help build your confidence to write in your journal is "I am free to write the reality of my life."

MUSIC

"Music takes me away."

We are often unaware of the profound and immediate effects of sound on our moods and behaviour. Sounds invigorate, frighten, soothe and trigger memories. If we want more peace and balance in our lives, we need to pay attention to the sounds surrounding us.

"When I'm feeling down, I play 'Into the Mystic' by Van Morrison. I made it through a few smoking urges this way."

The more artificial noises (machines, traffic, etc.) we live with, the more likely it is that we will experience difficulties relaxing. Human sounds can also be distressing. The voices of anger, hostility or frustration wear us down. Ongoing chatter, no matter how pleasant, will eventually overwhelm us. We often use smoking as a way to tune out the noise in our lives.

"People laugh when they see my apartment. No couch, no chairs, but a real nice stereo. It's my prized possession."

We need to strike a balance in our environments between sound and silence. We also need to immerse ourselves in the sounds of nature. Animal calls, the crashing of waves, the rush of the wind and the crackling of fire are ancient sounds, which nurture and restore.

Another abundant source of pleasure is music. Music is used in the journal exercises for its power to relax and soothe. It opens the heart, expands the mind, moves our bodies and transports us beyond our everyday reality. It's also a powerful tool to use to deepen the meditative state. With practice we can rely on music, instead of smoking, to lift our spirits.

It's a good idea to create a personal list of sounds and music that you like and dislike. Ask yourself how much time you spend surrounded by each of the different sounds listed. If you find you spend a lot of time with sounds and music that disturb you, this likely has a strong impact on any of your personal work—including your efforts to quit smoking. You can make a conscious effort to change this, by playing favourite music or retreating into a quiet place for a few minutes each day.

One of the most wonderful treats we can give ourselves is a home-made recording of our favourite songs on one tape. It's amazing how listening, singing along or dancing to our favourite songs can inspire and energize us.

"I don't know where I would be without my music. I love it."

What sounds/music do I dislike?

How much time each day do I spend with these sounds?

What sounds/music do I enjoy? (including silence)

How much time each day do I spend with these sounds?

Suggested Music for Relaxation, Writing and Pleasure

The best way to discover the music you enjoy is to spend some time listening to pieces at music stores. Many bookstores now carry a rich and diverse selection of tapes. (The library also loans out tapes and records—even CDs!!!) Ask the salespeople for assistance. Any recordings they do not have in stock can be located in catalogues and ordered. These are some of the favourite selections from Catching Our Breath group participants.

Relaxation & Meditation

The Crimson Collection
Mender of Hearts
Singh Kaur & Kim Robertson

Oriental Sunrise
Riley Lee, Gabriel Lee

Creative Visualization
Shakti Gawain

Pachelbel – Kanon with Nature's Ocean Sounds
Music for Relaxation and Tension Release
Invincible Records

Pachelbel for Relaxation
Chacra Alternative Music Inc.

The Fairy Ring
Mike Rowland

Much Silence
Gershon Kingsley

San
Chaitanya Hari Deuter

Tarashanti
Georgia Kelly

Tibetan Bells II
Henry Wolf,
Nancy Hemings

When You Wish upon a Star: Relaxation Music for Children
Li-Sem Enterprises Inc.

Rhythms of the Sea,
Eight Piano Moods
Dan Gibson's Solitudes

Writing & Pleasure

Deep Breakfast
Ray Lynch

A Rainbow Path
Kay Gardner

Ten Years
Kitaro

Watermark
Shepherd Moons
The Memory of Trees
Enya

You Are the Sea
Gilead Limor

The Visit
Loreena McKennitt

Medicine Man
Bobbie McFerrin

Music for the Native Americans
Robbie Robertson and The Red Road Ensemble

hi, how are you today?
Ashley MacIssac

Fire in the Snow
Rose Vaughan Trio

solo para ti
Ottmar Liebart & Luna Negra

Bach by the Sea
Gentle Persuasion

Up Where We Belong
Buffy Saint Marie

Sounds of Nature

Harmony
Exploring Nature with Music
Hennie Bekker, Dan Gibson

O'Cean
Larkin

River of Life
Jonathon Storm

The Singing Humpbacks
Marine Mammal Fund
Voices of Nature Series

Sounds of the Tropical Rain Forest
The Sounds of Nature
Essex Entertainment

Classical

Each of the following classical selections has been recorded by a variety of orchestras from around the world. The price of the tape or CD varies greatly. Ask your music or bookstore salesperson to help you choose the production that suits your taste and price range.

Albinoni
Adagio for Strings in G Minor

Beethoven
Moonlight Sonata
(Piano Sonata No. 14)
Für Elise

Gluck
Dance of the Blessed Spirits (from a larger piece *Orpheus and Euridyce*)

Handel
Royal Fireworks
Water Music

Mozart
Piano Concerto No. 21

Christopher Parkening
(guitar)
A Bach Celebration

Schubert
Unfinished Symphony

Sibelius
The Swan of Tuonela
Finlandia

Richard Strauss
Four Last Songs

Antonio Vivaldi
Concertos for Lute
Concertos for Mandolin
The Four Seasons

CREATING A SPACE

While working with this journal, it might also be a good time to think about creating a special place in your home for yourself. Creating a private space, like "journalling," sends a loving message to your inner self. It establishes you as a priority. Many women have a

"I said, 'You have got to be kidding. A space for myself in a big family like mine? Not likely!' But I found a little wooden shelf at a garage sale for three bucks. I put it up high on my wall and put some beautiful stones on it and a picture of me when I didn't smoke. I look at that shelf a few times a day and I think, 'Yeah, there's going to be a time again when I don't smoke.' That little shelf reminds me I'm worth taking care of."

difficult time doing this. We've been taught to serve others before ourselves, so it often feels selfish to take something (just) for ourselves.

One way to practise nurturing ourselves is to set aside a drawer, a corner or an entire room for ourselves. We might need to lock this place to keep it private or out of the reach of children. Remember you deserve this space! If you don't have the room to make a space for yourself, then keep a drawer or shelf for your special things.

When you work with the journal, clear a space for yourself. You may have a special cloth that you spread on your table, or a special pillow to sit on. It does not have to be elaborate to be your own. It helps to light a candle or burn incense or potpourri to create an atmosphere of calm.

REWARDS

"The best reward I can think of right now is going to bed a half hour earlier so I can read. I like inspirational stories about women's lives."

Following each of the exercises in the journal is a suggestion that you reward yourself in some way for the work you've completed. As smokers we often use our cigarettes to reward ourselves. If we want to quit smoking, learning new ways to nurture ourselves is very important and not something frivolous we can overlook. If we don't develop alternate rewards, we can easily slip back into thinking we deserve a cigarette.

Even though you will be doing some of these exercises as a smoker, you can experiment with rewarding yourself with something other than a cigarette. It's a good idea to develop your own list of treats and rewards. This practice will help you expand your ideas of self-care and eventually make the shift to healthier methods of self-care.

"My favourite reward is beautiful-smelling hand lotion. It gives me something to do with my hands and reminds me of how nice my hands look without cigarette stains on them."

For a variety of reasons one of easiest things to turn to is food. It's best to be compassionate with yourself about eating. Many women can be pretty hard on themselves for gaining weight, and no one needs that issue to sabotage efforts to quit smoking. Finding rewards other than smoking may take some extra effort, but this is much healthier overall. *The Woman's Comfort Book* by Jennifer Louden is an excellent resource. Here are a few ideas to get you started.

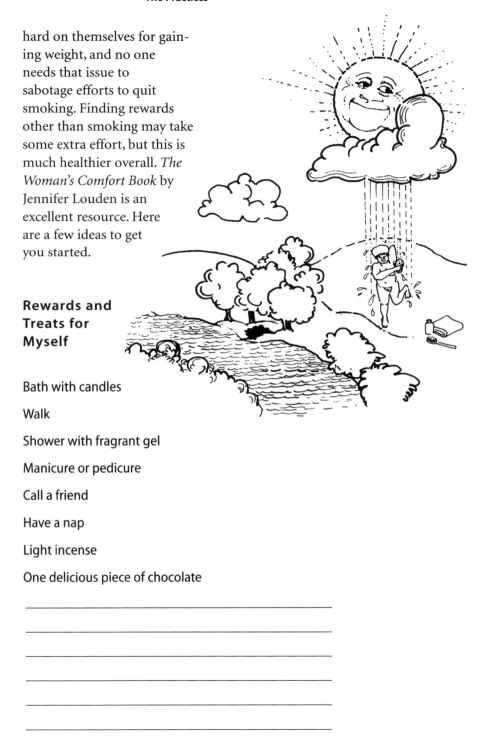

Rewards and Treats for Myself

Bath with candles

Walk

Shower with fragrant gel

Manicure or pedicure

Call a friend

Have a nap

Light incense

One delicious piece of chocolate

_____

_____

_____

_____

_____

_____

Culture and Tobacco

How did it come to be that people smoke? Was it always this way? Who smokes today? As smokers, we may have asked ourselves these questions. Smoking is so much a part of our lives that it is hard to imagine a world without cigarettes. Yet, smoking as we know it has only been practised for the past 100 years. There was a time when tobacco was used in completely different ways. Even today, most of the people in the world get through their day without cigarettes. It has taken many years and much effort to make smoking the addiction that it is now.

TRADITIONAL USE

The large and leafy tobacco plant is native to tropical America but can be grown in cooler climates. Some researchers believe that the plant has been cultivated here for over 8,000 years. It's possible that the ancient Maya introduced the plant to North

American Aboriginal peoples, who honoured the plant for its medicinal properties.

There are several beautiful stories and teachings of how the Creator instructed Native people to grow, prepare and use the plant for spiritual purposes. Many of the stories forewarned of the illness, suffering and death that would befall humans if they misused tobacco. Some of these teachings forbid humans to inhale the smoke or use tobacco for amusement.

People treated the plant with a great deal of respect. The smoke from tobacco that was burnt on sacred fires carried prayers to the spirit world. Tobacco was left on the earth as an offering of thanks. It was carried in medicine bundles or given as a special gift. The practices varied according to the people and their ceremonies.

For thousands of years, medicine men and women carefully cultivated the plant, picking it at exactly the right time and curing it naturally in the sunlight. It would then be blended with other plants native to the area, such as sage (often used in women's rituals), lavender, sassafras or sweetgrass, to be smoked during rituals and ceremonies.

The Cree mixed tobacco with a variety of other plants and named the mixture "kinnikinnik." As children matured, parents and grandparents taught them how to grow and mix tobacco. These teachings were carefully shared. Elders made clear the spiritual value of the plant and cautioned against thoughtless use of tobacco.

The Native healers who grew and blended the tobacco recognized the powerful effects on both mind and body when it was smoked. In their research, writers Donna Cunningham and Andrew Ramer (1989) found that:

"I feel heartened to know that a long time ago tobacco had a very different place in Native culture than it does today. I draw strength from the traditional teachings. They are helping me quit my addictive use of tobacco."

Fire was recognized by the ancients as a changer and releaser of the power of certain substances. . . . Thus the ancients burned or smoked a variety of things. Tobacco was only one, a stimulant, but there were also depressants. There were plants smoked for different parts of the body, healing and balancing them. There were different smokes for different folks and for different times of the year, depending on what was needed for that season. . . .

Like so much else, all of this was to change when the Europeans made contact with First Nations people in the 1400s. The Europeans immediately recognized the importance of tobacco in Native culture, even if they did not understand the spiritual meaning behind its use. Explorers and traders quickly began exploiting the value of tobacco as an important trade good.

The Hudson's Bay Company and the North West Company "gave" tobacco and alcohol in so-called "gift-giving" ceremonies to attract Native people into trading with them. Natives and Europeans began smoking tobacco together to seal their trade agreements or in honour of the new relationship between the two groups (Reading 1996).

Native people made a distinction between their original "true tobacco" that they grew themselves and the tobacco grown in South America and imported by Europeans. They continued to use their own tobacco in religious ceremonies and began using the imported tobacco for recreational purposes (Reading 1996).

At the same time, Europeans were taking up the habit of recreational smoking. Columbus is claimed to have introduced the tobacco plant to Spain. It soon became available in other countries. During the 1500s "tobacco-houses" were established for

"I think I would have felt really different about smoking if I knew how powerful tobacco was."

"I remember reading about a woman who described her cigarettes as medicine. I thought, 'You know, she's on to something.' It's true that tobacco is a medicine. But you can't benefit from a medicine if you take it without wisdom. It can kill you if you use it the wrong way."

"Columbus really screwed up."

35

> **"Knowing more about colonization and abuse is helping me understand all kinds of addictions."**

smokers in Europe and pharmacies sold tobacco on prescription only (Greaves 1996). It took over 300 years before we realized the terrible price everyone would pay for the corruption of the tobacco plant.

We now know that the government's ban of all traditional ceremonies made it almost impossible for Native people to use tobacco in their traditional ways. But the traditional teachings about tobacco were never lost. To this day, thousands of Native people use this sacred plant in rituals and ceremonies. It is still given as a gift to honour teachers and elders. It continues to be burned in fires during sweat lodges and used in prayer. Aboriginal children are being taught the ceremonial use of tobacco. Native organizations have established seed banks to replenish the supply of indigenous plants, so that Native people can once again grow and cure their own tobacco (see the listing for TNAT under "Organizations" at the end of the book).

> **"I'm growing my own tobacco and I will use it in ceremonies."**

Aboriginal elders never meant for tobacco to be used as a crutch to get through the day. They would be horrified by the mass production of cigarettes by multinational companies and the devastation it causes to people and our earth.

RECREATIONAL USE

By the 1800s smoking became a common social practice and people were beginning to connect certain illnesses with smoking. Canadian researcher and writer Lorraine Greaves has described how women were key in forming anti-smoking groups during the late 1800s and early 1900s, such as the National Anti-Cigarette League and the Non-Smokers Protective League of America. In Canada, the Women's Christian Temperance Union named the problem the "Cigarette Evil" (Greaves 1996).

These groups advocated for clean air and restriction of tobacco sales to children and warned of the health consequences of smoking. They wanted the government to ban the importing and manufacturing of cigarettes, but they were unsuccessful. They were able to affect public policy and develop educational campaigns (Greaves 1996).

The campaigns were mainly directed at men because it was mostly privileged males who smoked. The small percentage of women who smoked were considered of "poor character." But by the early 1900s this was starting to change. The anti-smoking groups were not powerful enough to counter the general population's growing interest in smoking. New developments in technology made it possible to mass-produce cigarettes. The tobacco industry needed to turn more people into consumers in order to make a profit.

"It amazes me to see how influenced we all are by our society and how hard it is to resist trends, like smoking. Nobody really knew what they were getting into."

Women represented a huge potential market for the tobacco industry. One of the ways the industry was able to capture the attention of women was to connect smoking with social changes that were dear to women's hearts and souls. Smoking was equated with smashing old rules that kept women down. Cigarettes were linked to important freedoms like women winning the vote. Smoking became a symbol of adventure and boldness (Greaves 1996).

Women who embodied these qualities were used to sell cigarettes. The famous pilot Amelia Earhart appeared in advertisements for Lucky Strike cigarettes in 1928, although she did not smoke. Movie stars graced the screens with cigarettes in hand, reinforcing the idea that smoking was glamorous and sophisticated.

"It kind of bugs me that even doctors used to smoke and now people act like you gotta be some kind of dummy to smoke."

Parts of society linked smoking with "masculine" behaviour and believed smoking appealed more to lesbians. The tobacco industry knew that for smoking to become popular, it needed to be thought of as part of a courting ritual between men and

women. The Chesterfield company set out to convince women that buying Chesterfields for a man would help to catch him as a husband. Their ad read "After a man's heart . . . when smokers find out the good things Chesterfields gives them, nothing else will do."

In the 1940s the tobacco industry was even able to exploit women's deep worry and sense of powerlessness over World War II. Tobacco companies encouraged women to ship cigarettes to soldiers overseas as a gesture of patriotism. In the 1950s, when women's roles were being restricted to that of wife and mother, the tobacco industry promoted smoking as an important leisure activity for "traditional" moms.

Tobacco companies continue to use advertising as a way to exploit our longing for friendship, adventure, individuality, freedom, courage and wealth by associating these things with smoking. Even good health has been linked to smoking! The Philip Morris company promotes its cigarettes with the slogan "You've come a long way baby!" suggesting smoking is one of the freedoms women have achieved. Of course, claiming that an addiction is in any way liberating is absurd.

Complete reversals of the truth are at the core of all cigarette advertising. A recent example is the portrayal of white, rich professionals enjoying cigarettes over brunch. In reality, these individuals are the least likely to smoke. Another advertisement tries to convince us that smoking will keep us thin and healthy. It shows a slim, beautiful woman on the beach. The caption reads "When a woman is wearing

"The advertisements make you feel that if you smoke you'll be just as thin, glamorous and rich as the people in the ads."

a bathing suit, there's no such thing as constructive criticism."

The young are the most vulnerable to believing messages that equate beauty, adventure and material success with smoking because they are still forming their own identities. The tobacco industry doesn't want to miss the chance to offer some suggestions about what it means to be a woman. It wants girls to believe smoking is a good way to cope with the stress of growing up. The industry knows that once girls are over 18, they rarely choose to take up the habit.

The industry also knows that smoking is losing popularity. It is highly motivated to find new smokers. By the 1970s the tobacco industry was aiming its campaigns at women and children. It introduced low-tar, low-nicotine, "light" cigarettes. The industry hoped these cigarettes would be easier for a young girl's body to tolerate. It knew that stronger brands made girls feel sick and discouraged them from smoking. The "light" and "slim" cigarettes appealed to women for different reasons. Low-tar cigarettes somehow seemed like a "healthy" alternative, which might even keep women slim (Greaves 1996)!

"How typical that the tobacco industry would advertise to sell their products while ignoring all the health facts about smoking."

Later, the tobacco industry moved on to promote cigarettes to specific ethnic and racial groups. It developed special brand names for cigarettes which it thought would appeal to African Americans and Hispanics. In the United States, over 90% of the billboards advertising cigarettes are in Black or Latino neighbourhoods (Greaves 1996).

Tobacco companies exploit the fact that gays and lesbians are discriminated against by mainstream culture. The industry has developed advertising which connects smoking with the freedom to be gay or lesbian. It thinks gays and lesbians will feel grateful for these ads and this will result in increased tobacco sales (Greaves 1996).

> "I think cigarette companies are only in it for the almighty buck. It sickens me to remember how they are now pushing cigarettes to the Third World countries."

Tobacco companies are now finding it easier to promote cigarettes in Third World countries, where there are few laws regulating tobacco and where people do not always know the health consequences of smoking. Cigarettes are often represented as symbols of "development" and are associated with the luxuries people enjoy in North America. In many countries around the world, free cigarettes are handed out at rock concerts. Art and cultural events and televised concerts of famous stars like Madonna are sponsored by tobacco companies.

Tobacco companies not only try to sell cigarettes to women, they use them as workers in the production of cigarettes (Greaves 1996). In many countries women plant, pick and cure tobacco leaves. They often do the heaviest work but get paid far less than men. Women suffer from nausea, dizziness and increased miscarriage as a result of the pesticides and the nicotine in the plants. Many women work in tobacco fields with their babies on their backs.

> "I feel kind of mad that the tobacco companies are making so much money off us women on low incomes ... and we're the ones that are getting sick too."

The production of cigarettes, including the growing of tobacco, often supplants the growing of food crops which are less profitable for farmers to cultivate. It requires large amounts of pesticides which rob the soil of its nutrients and put poisons in our ecosystem. It destroys thousands of trees (one tree per 300 cigarettes),which are cut down and burned for the curing process. The outcome of this process is a cigarette which contains over 4,000 toxic chemicals, many of which are known to cause cancer (Canadian Council on Smoking and Health 1989).

WHO SMOKES TODAY?

By 1964 smoking levels reached their peak. About 60% of men and 33% of women in Canada were smokers. At the same time the first reports linking smoking with serious illnesses were published. Since then, there has been a steady decrease in smoking among both men and women. However, men have been quitting at a faster rate than women, so the gap between the sexes is now closing. In 1994, 29% of women smoked compared to 32% of men (Health and Welfare Canada 1994).

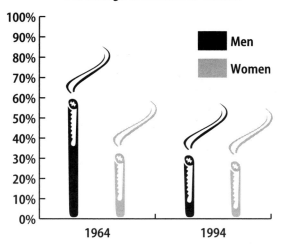

Percentage of Smokers in Canada

Another important gender difference occurs with the young. The number of girls smoking has risen over the past five years. It is estimated that 29% of teenage girls use tobacco compared to 26% of teenage boys. A number of factors, including advertising directed at females, mean the majority of these girls will form an addiction to cigarettes and are not as likely to quit as boys. It is feared that if this trend continues, women's smoking rates may actually surpass men's for the first time in history.

Smoking rates remain extremely high among Aboriginal people. The rates vary by region and nationhood, but overall 57% of First Nations and Métis adults are current smokers. Inuit women have the highest rate at 80%. Dene women are next at 65%. Non-Native women living in the same region have a smoking rate of 39%.

Smoking rates vary according to people's age. The highest rates are for people in the 20 to 24 age group, with 40% smoking. The levels in this age group are also highest for Aboriginal smokers. A study in the Northwest Territories in 1989 found that by age 19, 71% of Inuit were smokers, compared to 43% of non-Native youth (Health Canada 1995).

Those of us who are unemployed smoke more than employed women (42% vs. 31%). If we work in

"I don't like how much the attitude toward smoking has changed in our society. Now just about anyone—even strangers—think they can say anything to a smoker. Like this guy I don't even know says 'You have got to be some kind of idiot to smoke.' I was so angry I said, 'Yeah, and I heard being an asshole can give you a heart attack.'"

"I can see why having a tough job makes you smoke. I always smoke more when I'm working somewhere I hate."

41

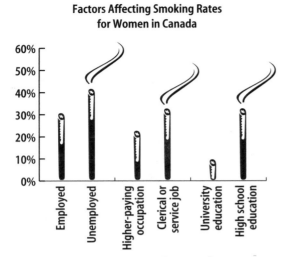

Factors Affecting Smoking Rates for Women in Canada

clerical or service jobs like waitressing, we smoke more than women in higher-paying occupations (33% vs. 23%). The more education people have, the less likely they are to smoke. Only 10% of university-educated women smoke compared to about 33% of those with some high school education. In Quebec in 1991, women were more likely to be daily smokers than men.

Francophone women and girls begin using tobacco at earlier ages and smoke more than Anglophones. If we live with smokers or if our parents smoked when we were growing up, we are also more likely to smoke (Canadian Council on Smoking and Health 1989).

Around the world about 30% of women in industrial countries smoke, but as in Canada there are huge differences depending on region, age, class and race. "In Third World countries about 2 to 10% of women smoke. In Africa 10% of women smoke, between 10 and 40% of Latin American women smoke, about 5% of South East Asian women smoke, 8% of Eastern Mediterranean women and less than 10% of Western Pacific women smoke" (Greaves 1996).

Research shows that not all women and men are at equal risk for starting to smoke or continuing to smoke. Our families, education, employment status, race and class each influence our dependence on cigarettes. These factors are worth exploring but are beyond the scope of this journal. For our purposes it is important for us to know that society's unfair treatment of individuals often creates personal and political conditions which may lead many people to smoke.

Initiation

Most of us began smoking when we were somewhere between the ages of 12 and 14. These years were difficult for many of us. There were so many things to think about. To begin with, our bodies were becoming visibly female. Starting our periods and growing breasts meant we were irrevocably entering into the world of women. We may not have understood the physical changes we were going through, let alone the emotional changes. The combination of hormones and our personal experiences probably meant that most of our time was spent madly fluctuating between laughing and crying.

Learning how to be a woman was an extremely confusing task. It was even more difficult if we were struggling to escape an abusive situation at home or if we had been sexually abused. Our experiences did not teach us to respect our bodies. Instead of celebrating who we were becoming, we were always trying to measure up or comparing ourselves with others.

We turned to cigarettes as a way of meeting our

needs and fulfilling our desires. Our society did a good job of teaching us that smoking helped people deal with stress, that it was one of the ways adults socialized, that it looked sophisticated and was fun! Other drugs adults use, such as alcohol and marijuana, might have also been appealing, but in most cases cigarettes are more accessible to a 13-year-old. Smoking made sense for those of us seeking relief or escape.

"I have lots of good memories about starting to smoke. I'm still friends with the girls I learned to smoke with. We were spunky and fiercely loyal to each other. Smoking was our pact. I've had to tell myself that we still would have been friends—even if we didn't smoke."

"When I started smoking at 12, it was to belong and be like an adult. It was to retaliate against my parents, family; to be my own person; to make choices for me. It gave me a 'high.' I wish I would have realized how powerful cigarettes are."

If we were feeling hurt or lonely we turned to our cigarettes for solace. If we were trying to be different from other girls, cigarettes became a symbol of rebellion. If we wanted to feel like we belonged somewhere, smoking with our friends symbolized intimacy and membership in a group.

We were also searching for a way to channel some of the intensity of our lives. Trying to keep our strong emotions and energetic bodies from running away with us was a daily challenge. We craved adventure! We wanted to feel the excitement life could offer. But for most girls there weren't enough

"Smoking gave me a power ... I think. It was something I chose. I wasn't told to do it. I became an adult in my mind fitting into the role that had been thrust upon me by my mother's death."

44

positive opportunities for thrilling escapes that might help us learn more about who we were. We had to settle for what was available—and for many of us this meant smoking. Lighting up a cigarette sent a powerful message to the world. Smoking meant we were leaving behind our childhood and entering into adulthood—at least symbolically.

For many of us smoking was a kind of rite of passage we shared with others. Maybe our circle of girlfriends became the safe community where we could talk about our deepest feelings and get support. Learning to smoke with our girlfriends was a way of acknowledging intimacy and a sense of belonging. Smoking was a "bad" enough activity to qualify as a risky behaviour and at the same time it felt safe to do. So, it was easy to use smoking as a way to break the rules and to build trust between friends by doing it together. Smoking became powerfully linked to a sense of closeness, friendship and adventure.

We probably didn't think too much about how the drug nicotine was affecting our bodies or that it was an extremely addictive substance. When we take a drag off a cigarette, the nicotine we inhale takes only about seven seconds to reach our brains. If we injected a drug it would take about 20 seconds to reach our brains. The cigarette is an extremely effective delivery system. The stimulant effects of nicotine are felt almost immediately. If we don't get sick or dizzy, we get a noticeable "head buzz." Nicotine triggers the release of adrenaline (which increases heart rate and blood pressure), acetycholine (which helps us relax) and endorphins (which gives us a sense of well-being).

As powerful as they are, the physical effects of nicotine are only part of the reason we get addicted to smoking. We all know friends who tried smoking in their teens but didn't get hooked. Our addiction to cigarettes is created by a combination of factors:

> "Once Mom ran out of cigarettes and she knew I smoked. She asked me for one. I felt approval."

> "I can remember the novelty of sneaking out with friends to light up. Adult behaviour was part of the pull—wanting to be grown-up but not knowing how to stop feeling needy. I often felt I wanted to be a little girl again. At least I knew my role. The new role seemed vague to say the least. You begin monitoring all your behaviours—your clothes, your hair. Somehow, no matter the care taken, I never looked good enough. Smoking helped me to forget myself, my inadequacies, my insecurity. I was behaving as if I was no longer a child. I could pretend I was grown-up."

the effects of nicotine on our bodies

our feelings at the time we tried smoking (excitement, fear, anxiety or whatever)

our environment—what was going on in our lives at the time we tried smoking

the particular circumstances in which we had our first cigarettes

our expectations about what smoking could give us.

If we liked what we felt, or if it seemed that smoking really did help us belong to a group or cope with our emotions, we created a strong relationship with the cigarette. We came to think of our cigarettes as helpers or friends. We mistakenly believed that smoking gave us the ability to contain our emotions or to feel better. Smoking became tightly woven into all of our daily activities. We started to depend on the cigarettes to cope with our lives. We became addicted.

Writer and researcher Alan Marsh studied 2700 smokers in Britain and found that the belief in smoking as a way of controlling our emotions is a key factor in getting hooked. He said:

> What the smoking adolescent never has the chance to learn is that like his non-smoking friends, he would have acquired that knack of affect control anyway. It is called growing up and nearly everyone does it, without the help of cigarettes. But he passes into adulthood firm in the belief that his ability to top and tail the range of his emotional responses depends on his daily intake of nicotine. Smoking is a *learned* experience (Marsh 1984).

Being young is the most significant risk factor in starting to smoke. Few adults ever choose this habit. But when an adult does start smoking, it is often during a life transition or significant turning point. And like adolescence, this turning point involves

"What I really wanted was love. I settled for smoking."

"My mother tried to persuade me to give it up. I think the support I needed most was my mother's understanding of my transition to being a woman."

"My rite of passage ceremony would have said one really strong message: Girls Are Great! Just that would have made a big difference."

46

trying to form a new identity, fit into a group or cope with a stressful situation.

Looking back to our initiation to tobacco can help us know why we developed such a strong attachment to smoking. We can see what smoking symbolized for us and how we might still believe the same misconceptions about smoking that we believed when we were young and vulnerable. Taking another look at why smoking appealed to us, but this time through our "adult eyes," can give us a more accurate picture of what smoking can and cannot give us. Looking back, we can see what we *really* needed and wanted.

"I want to be the kind of wise grandmother who can mentor her grand-children in how to live life positively, without addic-tions. Maybe I'll make a rite of passage for my daughter."

JOURNAL ENTRY: INITIATION

Prepare your space. Light a candle or burn incense. Begin with the relaxation exercise or a few minutes of conscious breathing. Play music if you wish. When you are ready, take a few minutes to reflect on the time of your own initiation to tobacco. You may want to find a photograph of yourself at the age you were when you began smoking, to help you remember. Music can also help remind you of this time. Try playing a piece of music that was important to you when you started smoking. Respond to these questions:

What kinds of things were going on in my life at this time?

How did I feel about myself?

Initiation

What was my self-esteem like?

How did smoking make me feel?

What needs was I trying to meet through smoking?

What did smoking symbolize for me?

What might have prevented me from turning to cigarettes? What would I like to say to my younger self?

How can I use what I know about my initiation to smoking to help me prepare to quit?

Our initiation to tobacco often happens at a difficult time during our lives. Remembering how we started smoking can also bring back other memories which might be painful. If you find this happening when you are writing, you can stop the exercise or you can continue to write, including your feelings about other experiences. If you feel overwhelmed by your feelings, call someone you can trust for support. Remember to breathe. You only need to remember or write about as much as you feel comfortable with. Try creating an affirmation that honours your strength and ability to cope. Above all, be gentle and loving with yourself.

After the exercise, reward yourself.

Awareness

Our reasons for smoking now might seem quite different from the ones that got us started. More than likely, we have rejected any notions that smoking makes us more sophisticated or exciting and may now believe we are driven to cigarettes by addiction alone. But cigarettes still remain symbols—just some of the wants and needs they represent have changed.

Smoking still symbolizes membership in a certain group. Smoking might be the way we establish a bond with others like us—especially if we are part of a minority or marginalized group. Smoking might be common where we live. We might find ourselves living in an environment where offering cigarettes is viewed as a gesture of kindness or generosity. Helping others feel comfortable in difficult situations and welcomed in a group is a deed worth cherishing. But we can express the same values through good communication skills instead of by sharing cigarettes.

Since smoking is a misguided attempt to meet needs and to fill the empty places in our lives, the

"Smoking in my life today is more bother than not! I work in a smoke-free building and most places are non-smoking these days. So I find I have to go outside and hide by myself. I guess this fits my life because I hate my job environment and it's an excuse to go off and be by myself."

more we know about what we want, the more able we are to respond in other ways. We can address our needs directly rather than relying on nicotine for a quick fix. After all, cigarettes alone cannot make us happy or relaxed. We do this for ourselves. For example, at the same time we light up a cigarette we also tell ourselves something like, "Okay, you can relax now," or "You can focus on your work now," or whatever else we need to tell ourselves. These reassuring messages are healthy, but obviously the smoking we have learned to associate with them is not. It is possible to separate the two. We can learn to let go of our cigarettes while keeping the ability to give ourselves encouragement and support.

This process of going inside of ourselves to find what we need is sometimes described as "getting centred." This simply means clearing our heads, relaxing and calming or reassuring ourselves. The opposite of feeling centred would be feeling confused, stressed, anxious or flipped out. For smokers, lighting a cigarette is a fast way of getting centred.

If we are going to quit smoking we need to find other ways to get centred. The first step is to pay attention to all the ways we use cigarettes. In some traditions of meditation, paying close attention to our environment, thoughts and actions is called *mindfulness*. Mindfulness gets us in touch with both our inner and outer environments. Not only do we notice the chatter in our heads, we also notice how the people around us, our jobs and our relationships affect us.

We need to practise mindfulness as smokers. When we do, we see that no thought or action (including smoking) comes out of the blue. Each can be traced back to a source. We may find we smoke more around people who make us feel angry and less around those with whom we feel happy—or the opposite. When we tune in to our lives, we may

"The pressure of university is off now. I'm feeling more space and relaxation now. This is likely a good time to quit."

discover we can go for long periods without smoking when we are doing the things we love. We may find we reach continuously for a cigarette to push down our anger in an argument. Smoking might be a way of blocking out emotions. If we are bored or lonely, we may use our cigarettes to help pass time. We might be surprised to discover that only a few of our cigarettes are smoked simply to satisfy a strong craving for nicotine. Whatever our situation, finding out why we smoke will help us quit.

Paying attention to when we smoke also helps us to place our addiction in a wider context. We can see that if we are working outside the home and raising children (and 62% of women with children are), we are doing double shifts, spending 90 to 100 hours per week in total on our outside and inside jobs. Smoking is often how we cope with the demands of this type of life.

We can also see why poverty and smoking are so closely linked. If we can't afford a babysitter or don't have access to a car or have no money for extras, smoking easily becomes our treat. But the truth is cigarettes don't make our lives easier; poor women who smoke are no happier than poor women who don't smoke.

Practising mindfulness helps us to make wise decisions about how we want to direct our energy. When we understand the source of our smoking urges, we are no longer at their mercy. Between the urge to smoke and the decision to light up is a small space. In that space lies our power to choose what to do. We can learn new ways of responding to our cravings for cigarettes. And we can begin to change the situation (like working too much, etc.) from which they arise.

"I smoke when I'm sad. The happier I am, the less I smoke."

"When do I smoke? ... when I finish some work, when I take a break, when I want to think about something, when I finish a meal, when I'm under pressure, feel stressed, arguing, when I read, play music, watch TV, when I drive, when I socialize, when I'm bored."

"I mostly smoke when I'm at home. I can go a whole day at work without smoking."

CRAVINGS AND CUES

Discovering your triggers and cues is very helpful in quitting. Make a list of the situations in which you usually find yourself wanting to smoke.

What kind of cigarette is it?

You might find it useful to describe your cigarettes in the following ways:

1 Aid
This cigarette helps you focus, relax or get through a situation.

2 Automatic
This cigarette is smoked because it is there, you didn't give smoking it much thought.

3 Addiction
This cigarette is smoked because you are craving the nicotine.

For each situation that you've written above, decide which category fits.

JOURNAL ENTRY: AWARENESS

Prepare your space. Light a candle or burn incense.
Begin with the relaxation exercise or a few minutes of
conscious breathing. Play music if you wish.

When you are ready, start writing about how you think
smoking fits into your life. Ask yourself:

What are all the things I am doing in my life right now?

How does smoking fit in?

What would I have to change in order to quit?

Do I feel this is a good time for me to quit smoking?

What does smoking symbolize for me?

When you are finished the exercise, give yourself a
reward.

Change

Smoking is more than an addiction to nicotine. It is a deeply ingrained behaviour. Smoking is part of our body language, just like walking or talking. Having a cigarette has meaning in the same way other types of gestures and motions have meaning. We use it to signal a "time out" from our children. We offer cigarettes to other smokers in friendship or to "break the ice" in unfamiliar situations. The expression "Let's have a cigarette" has many different meanings, including "It's time to celebrate," or "Stop talking." We light up to claim a space for ourselves and warn off people we don't want to be with. In threatening situations, women have used smoking to diffuse conflict or to stall sexual advances.

We smoke when we are bored or need to distract ourselves. We reach for our cigarettes when we feel lonely, tired, angry or stressed. We smoke to fill the "empty spaces" in our lives and in ourselves. We rely on smoking to help give structure to our day. Cigarette breaks become resting or stopping places, where we punctuate tasks we have completed, reflect on how we're feeling and think about what we still have to do. Smoking becomes our way of organizing and marking time.

Because smoking is so tightly bound to everything we do in our lives, it becomes a part of who we are: our identity. And so, quitting is more profound than simply "not smoking." Quitting smoking involves reconsidering our whole *way of being* in the world. It requires us to rethink our values, our social relationships, how we spend our time and how we cope with our lives. Anyone who has tried to quit knows this is why it can be so difficult and exciting at the same time.

The process of quitting is a process of change. In quitting we gather valuable insights about ourselves and how we change, which we can apply in other areas in our lives. The changes we have already made, no matter how unrelated they may seem, will affect how we approach quitting. Thinking about quitting now is probably born out of these other changes. It could be that smoking no longer fits with who we are or are becoming. Whatever the circumstances, our success in staying off cigarettes will depend, in part, on how other realities shift and change.

Quitting, like any other significant change in our lives, is not something that happens in a straight line, with a clear beginning, middle and end. We will likely make several attempts at quitting before we become successful abstainers. In fact, it's very important to remember that; *most people who quit successfully tried anywhere from a couple to dozens of times before it worked. Each time you try to quit you get closer to letting go of your cigarettes for good.*

Think of quitting as a process rather than a goal. If we drew a picture of a process, it would look like a spiral. Imagine yourself as the pen that draws the spiral. Sometimes you will feel like you are going backwards or in circles. But each turn of the spiral is larger than the one before it, and while reaching into

> "At first I was angry that I had to do all this 'work' to get off cigarettes. I was angry that I got addicted in the first place. Then I thought, 'You know, if it weren't for trying to stop smoking, I might never have taken the time to really examine my life, to make other changes that have totally improved how I feel about myself and my relationships.'"

new places, it envelops the smaller circles already formed.

Since a detailed exploration of change could fill several journals (a list of books on the subject of change is included at the end of the journal), we will limit our discussion to five main aspects of change: how we approach change, where we are now, motivation, stages of change and the Smoker's Wheel of Change.

HOW WE APPROACH CHANGE

It has been said that change is the only constant in our lives. Change happens whether we invite it or not. Ultimately, there is no way to effectively resist change. Our power lies in how we choose to participate in and respond to change.

If we grew up in environments where we were not consulted or considered in decision making, we may have learned to regard change with distrust or a sense of helplessness. If the changes thrust upon us caused us grief or harm, we may continue to believe that all change is chaotic and bad. We may have come to the conclusion that we are no good at handling change. As a result, we cling to old behaviours and beliefs, even when these hurt us, compromising ourselves for the "devil we know over the devil we don't." Waiting for change to happen to us, without trying to manage it for ourselves, is a *reactive* way of responding.

If we grew up believing we had a say in matters, we probably learned how to participate in change. We likely felt that change could be good and that we had some power in managing it. When we make things happen for ourselves and try to influence change, we are responding *proactively*.

When we are proactive, we remain attentive and can anticipate change. We believe in our powers of influence and trust in our ability to cope with

"Some changes I have made: change in job, change in residence, change in living arrangements, started Sara in day care, changed attitude toward 'shoulds' in my life, changed responses to some people, stand up for my beliefs, will not accept negative humour about women."

"Clearly change is a necessary part of life. Changes that happen beyond my control are the most difficult to deal with. As a rule if I think of changes I am usually optimistic and invite a challenge—I view change as positive."

change positively. Those who are reactive or frightened of change are literally too scared to look. It's not surprising when they crash into the changes they were trying to avoid. This reinforces the belief that change is overwhelming and we are powerless.

We sometimes hesitate to take action to change because we have been taught that people should make changes in a decisive, "all-or-nothing" way, with no slips back to our old behaviours. Smokers often say, "I don't want to try quitting because I don't want to fail at it." We need to realize that each attempt at a new behaviour, including quitting smoking, carries with it false starts and setbacks.

> "I feel I'd like to make changes in my life.... However, I feel insecure and unloved at this time, which is barricading my hopes and dreams."

Relapses, or slips back to old behaviours, are part of the process of change and need to be viewed as opportunities to review and revise. Relapses alert us to our limitations and can stop us from doing too much too soon.

Relapses can also make us feel discouraged and cause us to doubt our ability to change. Many women report feeling burnt-out from change. Each of us goes through periods when we just don't feel strong enough to make another change, even though we believe that we could benefit from the change. This often happens because we don't understand the reasons behind our unwanted behaviour and have convinced ourselves that our failed attempts to change are proof that we are weak.

Talking with other women about our discouragement and frustration in trying to quit smoking can help us put things in perspective. We can see that others struggle with the same feelings and that even though we are individuals, we share many of the same obstacles to change. We begin to recognize that there are many factors that influence the direction of our lives and our choices.

Research from around the world shows that people's health differs widely depending on where they live, the gaps between rich and poor, and how valued they feel. The more choices we have, the more likely we are to change our behaviour, including smoking.

Many people have long understood the impact of realities such as violence and poverty on our health. For instance, the feminist movement has made explicit how the status of women in our world has affected our well-being and the choices we can make. There are many examples of how important social changes—such as winning the vote or the right to attend university—began with women coming together to talk about their personal experiences.

> "I have changed my social attitudes and I don't drink coffee anymore. I'm also looking at my family bonds and I'm trying to change the situation in a loving and positive way."

Change in our lives is supported when we come together to share our struggles, offer support and encouragement and learn from each other. In the case of smoking, we need to see how our culture legitimizes and promotes cigarettes while at the same time condemning smokers for being addicted.

Acknowledging the social forces that shape our decision does not diminish our personal power or shift the responsibility for change onto someone or something else. Learning more about how we are influenced can help us create a realistic plan for getting unaddicted.

Knowing more about how social conditions affect people's habits has convinced many that addictions are not "diseases" caused by our genes or our biochemistry. They are attempts to cope in a troubled world. Addictive behaviour is modelled to us by our families and our community. We use substances not because they are so irresistibly pleasurable, but because they are offered to us so we can escape from the world rather than change it.

It's also important to remember that many of the conclusions that have been drawn about how addictive a substance is have come from research done on animals living in cramped and unnatural environments.

> The inadequacy of such research has been demonstrated by a series of ingenious studies at Simon Fraser University in British Columbia. The researchers designed a spacious stimulating environment dubbed "Rat Park" in which male and female rats lived together; they then compared these animals with those housed in isolated cages. Unsurprisingly, the caged rats drank many more times of a sweetened morphine solution (in preference to water) than those living in Rat Park. Even after having been isolated and habituated to the drug, rats who then were given the opportunity to enjoy the space and companionship in Rat Park rejected the morphine solution almost completely in favour of water (Peele, Brodsky and Arnold 1991).

We are not destined to repeat the patterns of our family or our society. No matter how it used to be for us, we can learn to embrace change and work with it. Besides responding to change that happens to us, we can participate in *self-directed* change.

WHERE WE ARE NOW

There is no question that our current life situation affects how we change. If we feel safe, secure and loved, we are in a better position to be proactive about change than if we feel threatened, abandoned or unloved.

If, for example, we live in situations where we are abused and controlled, we are likely to behave reactively. It is estimated that one in 10 women is abused by her partner. Physical and emotional abuse in relationships causes women to put their energy into protecting and defending themselves. In these situations a woman's capacity to change is severely restricted. Abuse becomes a vicious cycle. The more we are abused, the more we feel incompetent and powerless, and the less we trust in our judgment to take action. The less action we take, the more likely we are to remain in abusive situations, and on and on it goes. The struggle to survive can drain us of our energy and enthusiasm for living.

On the other hand, living in a relatively stable and loving environment is no guarantee we will invite change into our lives or handle it well when it arrives unannounced. A predictable and comfortable life can make us smug and complacent. We may not want to endure the inevitable discomfort of change.

The truth is no matter who we are, jobs are won and lost, lovers come and go, and illness and death affect us. Smoking might feel like a buffer against these harsh realities, but it really isn't. Women who smoke are no happier or able to deal with crisis than women who don't smoke. Although it certainly makes good sense to choose a relatively calm time in our lives to attempt quitting, we need to be careful not to postpone quitting smoking for that "perfect" time that never arrives. Many women leaving abusive relationships (which is all by itself a profoundly proactive decision) have used this transition to make other significant changes, including quitting smoking. Other women have used the biological shifts in their lives, such as pregnancy, menopause or illness, as opportunities to quit.

There is no way to neatly decide what the limits for change are in any one situation. Sometimes it is precisely because of a terrible situation or crisis that we change. Have you ever noticed how just when you think there's no room for change, an opening appears?

MOTIVATION

A motivator is a force that causes us to act. We can describe motivators as either internal or external.

An internal motivator flows from our own desire to change. If we decide to quit smoking because we are worried about our health, we no longer enjoy the taste or the smell or we just don't want to be addicted to tobacco, we are acting upon internal motivators.

If, instead, we stop smoking because our friends or our family want us to, or because we can no longer smoke at home or work, or to receive a cash reward, external motivators are fuelling our change. The source of our motivation will affect how we move through a change, as well as how difficult or easy we find the change.

Since external motivation comes from a source outside, we may be responding to a demand we don't even agree with. We might say, "Okay, I'll quit smoking to stay in this relationship, but I don't think it's fair and I don't like the idea!"

When our attempts at change are based on someone else's ideas, or if they are done for rewards or praise from others, they're less likely to be successful. If the rewards or praise are withdrawn, it's easy to abandon the effort because it was never what we wanted in the first place. This is not to suggest that we stop looking for support, praise or information from others. These are helpful. But it is important that the impulse and the desire for change come from inside us.

To have lasting success, we need to believe in our own reasons for change and to please ourselves with our new behaviour.

"I remember watching the Boston marathon on TV and thinking, 'Wow!' It was seeing women in their 50s and 60s running that gave me the inspiration to quit smoking. I thought, 'Hell, if they can learn to run 26 miles non-stop at their age, it's not too late for me.' I'm 51, and I'm happy to say I'm smoke-free and loving it!"

JOURNAL ENTRY: CHANGE

Prepare your space. Light a candle or burn incense. Start with the relaxation exercise or a few moments of conscious breathing. Play music if you wish. When you are ready, begin writing. Ask yourself:

What does change mean to me?

How have I handled change in the past?

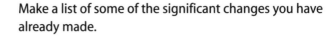

Make a list of some of the significant changes you have already made.

Read over the list and create an affirmation that honours your ability to change. For example, "I welcome change in my life," or "I have the power to create positive change in my life."

When you are finished the exercises, give yourself a reward.

STAGES OF CHANGE

Quitting smoking, or making any change, does not
happen all at once. We go through a process with
several stages. Writer and psychologist James
Prochaska (1994) has identified six stages of change.
He believes that in each stage we have important
tasks to complete before we move on to the next
stage. Prochaska believes that one of the reasons
popular quit-smoking programs aren't as successful
as they could be is that they are geared only to people in the action stage and miss providing support
and guidance to people in the other stages.

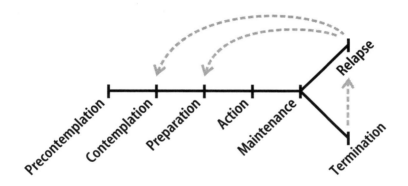

Precontemplation
In this stage we may not think we have a problem
and we don't have any intention of changing. We
may lack information about the consequences of our
behaviour.

Contemplation
As contemplators we know we have a problem and
we want to understand it. We have indefinite plans
to take action within six months or so. We need
more information on how to change.

Preparation
In this stage we are making a plan and getting ready

to take action within the next month. We may have already started making smaller changes.

Action
This is where we actually stop smoking. This is the stage where people can see the change, so we get more recognition here than during the other stages.

Maintenance
Maintaining our change is an ongoing process. We need to keep our commitment and stay focused on our new behaviours. This stage can last six months to a whole lifetime.

At this point we might terminate our habit for life or relapse.

Relapse
This means we start smoking again. It is a normal experience. It is common to relapse several times before we stay smoke-free.

Termination
This is the ultimate goal. Here we no longer feel any temptation to smoke and are confident that we won't relapse. Some experts believe that it is not possible to completely terminate certain problems. They believe we are always at risk for relapse.

People do not necessarily move through these stages one after another. Sometimes we get stuck in one stage or "recycle" through the stages. Knowing the stage we are in can help us understand what we need to do. We might relapse several times. Prochaska reminds us that "Experience with change strengthens people, and relapses most often take them not to precontemplation, but to contemplation or preparation, relatively close to making commitments to renewed action."

THE SMOKER'S WHEEL OF CHANGE

Another way to understand how change happens is
to think of the desired change—in this case quitting
smoking—as a wheel. The hub or centre of the
wheel and each spoke represent an important part of
the change.

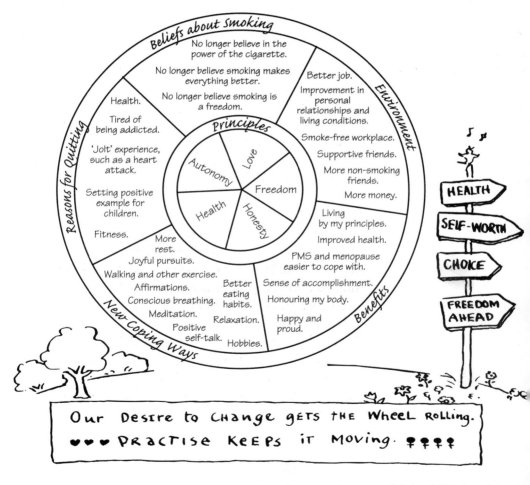

Our Desire to Change gets the Wheel Rolling.
♥♥♥ Practise Keeps it Moving. ♀♀♀♀

Principles

If we want to quit smoking, it helps to begin by reviewing the principles that are at the heart of this change. We need to know what we care about, what has truth and meaning for us, what we build our decisions around in life. If we don't believe life has meaning or purpose, why would we consider stopping an unhealthy habit? Our behaviours flow from our principles.

Women in Catching Our Breath groups have affirmed that they are guided by principles such as *love, honesty, wisdom, autonomy, respect, justice, integrity, health, humour, compassion and humility.*

Beliefs about Smoking

After years of associating smoking with everything else we do, we have taught ourselves to believe a powerful idea, fundamental to keeping us hooked: *Smoking makes everything better.* Stress seems easier to handle, good times seem more fun and everything feels more "complete" if we smoke. Nicotine helps us feel more alert and improves our ability to function.

Each cigarette we smoke reinforces this belief to the point that we attribute almost everything we do to the "power" of the cigarette to make it happen. *The truth is, a cigarette is just a cigarette.* It cannot protect us or ease our burdens. As we will discuss further in upcoming chapters, we do these things for ourselves.

Nicotine *is* a powerful drug which causes many biochemical changes in our bodies. Research now tells us that nicotine affects two main places in our brains: the limbic cortex, which is involved in feeling pain and pleasure; and the locus coeruleus, which is involved in stimulating us and giving us a sense of "being awake." Every time we take a drag off a cigarette we send nicotine to these centres in our brains, stimulating them and setting off a cascade of biochemical changes. In one study, various drugs such as caffeine and cocaine were given to street drug users without them knowing which drug they were receiving. When asked what drug was the most appealing, many of them chose the one that turned out to be nicotine (Krogh 1991)!

Although it helps us to know this so we don't underestimate the effect of nicotine on our brains, we should not be too overwhelmed or impressed by this information. After all, everything we do affects our biochemistry. And some experiences—like making love—are also extremely powerful biochemical experiences, but that doesn't mean we will become addicted to orgasms or have sex compulsively.

We find it difficult to give up smoking for lots of reasons, not just because of the biochemical "rewards" of nicotine. One of the reasons is that our bodies try to maintain a state of balance called *homeostasis*. When we introduce nicotine into our bodies we disrupt this balance, causing our bodies to seek a new level of homeostasis which accommodates nicotine.

Periods of smoking and then not smoking require our bodies to perpetually seek a new state of balance. In other words, it's not so much that we are more alert when we smoke, we're just not experiencing the fuzzy-headed feeling that comes from withdrawing from nicotine. Feeling more focused when we smoke is also due to factors such as positive self-talk and breathing, which we will discuss further in Chapters 9 and 10.

We can become so dependent on the temporary "focus" that smoking gives us that we downplay the fact that our cravings for nicotine frequently disrupt our concentration. How many times have we found it difficult to sit through a movie or finish a task because of a "nicotine fit"?

Many smokers give up cigarettes without ever really changing their belief that "smoking makes everything better." These ex-smokers tend to be unhappy about quitting. They are at serious risk for relapse, because they feel like they gave up something wonderful and powerful when they quit smoking. As obvious as it might sound, only people who are addicted to cigarettes think cigarettes are great and can make everything better.

Non-addicted people do not turn to smoking to feel better, despite the possible "benefits" of the stimulant nicotine. What separates the two groups is simply their *beliefs* about smoking. It's really worth the effort it takes to change these. One woman described this process as "de-brainwashing" herself. If we really want to be free of our addiction we need to stop believing in the power of the cigarette and view it more accurately as paper, tobacco, nicotine and 4,000 chemicals.

Reasons for Quitting

We have already discussed the importance of having our motivation to change come from within. Making a list of the reasons we want to quit smoking helps us in two ways.

"When I saw my beautiful little granddaughter pick up one of my butts, I felt sick. There's no way I want her to be a smoker. All of the women in my family smoke. I don't want another generation to start. Now, every time I get an urge to smoke, I think of her. It's going to be different for her."

First, it reinforces the fact that the decision to quit smoking *is personal and belongs to us*. Think about how passionately we feel about our personal "choice" to smoke. We don't want to be told what to do and how to do it. We know it is essential to make our own decisions. The same is true for quitting smoking. It's possible for us to redirect the passion we feel about our right to smoke into determination to quit. Our reasons for quitting can be just as private and unique as our reasons for smoking.

Second, creating a list of reasons for quitting gives us something to refer to during those difficult moments when we ask ourselves, "Why am I doing this?" It makes it easier to endure the discomfort of withdrawal and the feelings of loss if we have clear ideas about why we need to quit. We can draw strength from knowing quitting is "right" for us.

Here are some of the reasons for quitting women in Catching Our Breath groups have shared:

"My health will improve."

"I don't want to worry about cancer or heart disease."

"I'm tired of being addicted."

"I want to be a good role model for my kids."

"I want to follow traditional teachings about tobacco."

"I'm not giving any more money to those big companies."

"I want to be free!"

"It's time to take care of *me*!"

"I want to be a grandmother."

"I want to get fit and strong."

"I can't accept what smoking does to the environment."

"I don't need it. I can find something better to give myself."

Benefits

We are much more likely to maintain a change if we can see the benefits from it. Sometimes we don't realize or feel the benefits from quitting smoking right away. It often takes some time for our bodies to heal and our new "non-smoking self" to feel normal and natural. In the meantime, we can use visualization techniques and simple common sense to imagine the many benefits from quitting smoking. Some benefits, like not spending money on cigarettes, will be immediate. Here are some other benefits:

"Quitting smoking has given me the confidence in myself I needed to go back to school."

"I don't wake up coughing in the middle of the night."

"My kids are so proud of me!"

"I feel more in control."

"I like how I smell."

"I can actually walk up the hill to my house without wheezing!"

"I'm putting the money in a jar and buying new shoes with it."

"I feel happy, like I've really accomplished something."

"I'm not killing myself anymore."

"I'm honouring my body for the first time in my life!"

"I'm breathing better."

"I feel like a grown-up!"

"I'm not addicted."

"I can take an airplane without having a nic-fit."

Environment

"I promised myself that after I quit drinking, I would get to quitting smoking. I want to be completely free of addictions and healthy. But quitting smoking has been tough, because everyone in my AA group smokes. And not everyone appreciates me pointing out that smoking is an addiction too."

We already know how crucial it is to get support from our friends and family when we quit smoking. It is just as critical that we pay attention to other aspects of our environment. In Catching Our Breath groups we ask ourselves several key questions in order to get a better picture of what else might need to change to support quitting. After thinking and writing about these questions many women say, "Gee, I never realized how much certain situations in my life drain my energy. No wonder quitting smoking feels like just one more hard thing I have to do. I need to make myself a priority if I want to stop smoking." Of course it isn't that simple to change our environment. Even so, it helps us to know what we are up against and the situations to avoid. We need to be aware of how our environment supports or blocks our efforts to change.

Our work or living situation could be undermining our efforts to stop smoking. How much time do we spend in smoky places such as a coffee shop, the bar or the homes of friends who smoke? Are our jobs so stressful and demanding that having a cigarette is the only time we get a break? Is smoking the norm in our community? Is it possible to spend more time in smoke-free places? Researchers have documented that smoke-free spaces help us become and remain non-smokers.

Conditions in our environment that support us to quit smoking include:

"I have some wonderful non-smoking friends."
"I work in a non-smoking restaurant."
"I feel much better about myself now that I'm in school."
"Counselling is really helping."
"I love my new apartment. I don't want to smoke in it."
"It helped me to hear about the new studies on smoking and cervical cancer. I can't pretend smoking won't hurt me."
"I love my Catching Our Breath group. I'd come even if I wasn't a smoker!"
"I smoke way less since I left that horrible relationship."
"I'm happy that there isn't cigarette advertising smeared all over the place. Even though I think those ads are silly, just seeing a package of cigarettes would trigger a smoking urge."
"I appreciate all the non-smoking public spaces."
"I'm in an alcohol treatment program for women. Once I overcome my drinking problem, then I'll think about quitting smoking."

"Since I've lost my job I've been smoking more even though I don't have any money. I feel out of control. I used to say smoking was my choice, but it's really my addiction. I'm sick of feeling poor and powerless. Quitting will help me spend my money on what I want—not what wants me. I can do it!"

New Ways of Coping

We smoke in an effort to meet real needs. Becoming a non-smoker involves learning new ways to meet these needs directly, instead of through smoking. For example, if we smoke more when we are tired, maybe we need to get more sleep instead of relying on the stimulant effects of nicotine. This might involve other changes such as making our bedrooms or beds more comfortable or letting our families know how important it is they respect our sleeping times.

In the next chapters we will explore in more detail what smoking "gives" us and discuss simple but effective ways to cope with ourselves and our lives, instead of smoking. We have covered a few of these in Chapter 2. Women have said that they find the following new coping methods helpful.

"I deep breathe many times each day."
"I'm learning to go to bed on time and rest more."
"I actually bring a lunch to work now."
"Painting is my new passion."
"I practise positive self-talk. I say nice things to myself."
"I remind myself that smoking won't make it better."
"I find other ways of being bad that won't kill me."
"I have a song I sing in my head when I'm frightened. It helps me feel like I can protect myself."
"I take brisk walks."
"I take breaks."
"I say no when I don't want to do something."
"Bubble baths!"
"I read more."
"I started sewing gigantic stuffed rabbits. It keeps my hands busy."

The Smoker's Wheel of Change can help us identify what aspect of the change we still might need to develop. For example, we may have lots of good reasons for quitting and a supportive environment, but haven't practised enough new coping skills. We may find we simply don't know what to do instead of smoking. Or it could be that we have developed five of the six areas of change, but haven't really changed our belief about smoking. We still believe smoking makes everything better. So, instead of actually letting go of that idea, we use "willpower" to suppress it. Eventually stress or a crisis makes this impossible and we act on our belief that smoking can help us. We find ourselves reaching for a cigarette.

Try to think of your *desire to quit smoking* as the energy or the force that sets the Wheel of Change in motion. Now imagine what your wheel looks like. Is there a centre of strong principles that holds it together? Are there five strong spokes? What spokes need to be built or reinforced? How easy or difficult would it be to push your wheel or keep it rolling? Can you imagine how frustrating it would be to move a wheel that is missing spokes? Even an amazingly strong woman with a big desire to quit smoking would eventually give up from exhaustion.

Take some time to create your own Wheel of Change. Think about some of the "rough terrain" in your life that your wheel will move through. Remember that difficult life situations can damage or break our wheel. But rarely is the damage irreparable. Making a daily commitment to care for each of the aspects that make up our wheel keeps it strong.

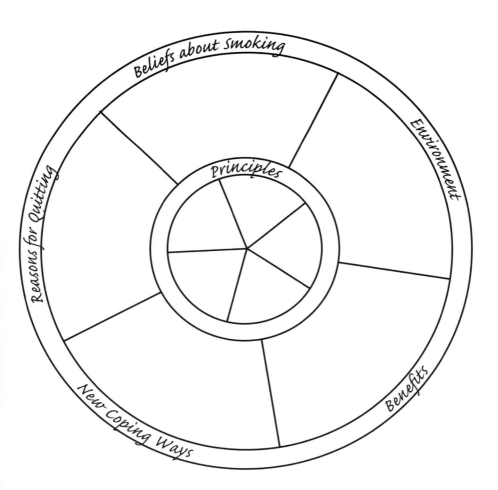

Freeing the Mind

No behaviour comes out of the blue. Each behaviour or action first begins as a thought. If we want to quit smoking we need to know what thoughts keep us reaching for a cigarette. Telling ourselves that "smoking makes it better" is certainly one of the most powerful thoughts in keeping us hooked. But there are others. We might be nurturing the thought that smoking is a way of taking care of ourselves or having fun. We might think that smoking will help us deal with our feelings. Each woman has her own set of thoughts or beliefs about what smoking can give her.

We experience these thoughts as "conversations in our heads." Another way of describing it is to call it *self-talk*. Self-talk can be negative or positive. A smoker's self-talk sounds something like this: "I need a cigarette," "I deserve a smoke break," "Yes! Finally some time for me," or "I'll feel better when I have a cigarette." Our self-talk is so constant that we lose awareness of it over time. It becomes the background noise as we go about our daily lives. We tend to forget that our thoughts have power and are determining our behaviours. Statements like "I can't quit" or "I need cigarettes" are examples of negative self-talk. These thoughts can prevent us from even attempting to quit smoking.

Many of the ideas that make up our self-talk originate from sources outside ourselves. They are opinions we hear in the media or at home or work. We kind of "absorb" them from our environment. For example, the belief that smoking makes life better wasn't our original idea. The tobacco industry has worked hard over the last 60 years to convince us that this is true. We can either reject this idea or let it take up space inside our heads and keep us hooked on cigarettes.

But there are more than just false messages about smoking cluttering our minds. Other media messages, which are unrelated to smoking, can also affect our addiction to cigarettes. A good example is the portrayal of women in advertising. Every day, we are overwhelmed with images that equate thinness with beauty, and largeness with ugliness. This drives many women to smoke to suppress their appetite and stay thin.

Of course, since time began, women have come in all different sizes and shapes. Thinking there is only one way to be acceptable—in this case thin—is an idea that doesn't reflect reality. It also doesn't reflect the reality of what it means to be healthy. It's simply an opinion. Just like the message about smoking, we can reject it or incorporate it into our self-talk.

When we hear ourselves say, "Look at how fat I am," we are participating in a very toxic form of self-talk. It makes us feel hateful towards ourselves and eats away at our resolve to remain non-smokers. In this state of mind, we can easily turn to cigarettes as a way of comforting ourselves and losing weight.

One effective way of dealing with negative self-

"It's true that most of the rubbish I've told myself never even came from me. It's from a nasty boy in Grade Six, or the media or some other place. Why the heck I ever listened to those ideas, I'll never know."

"The idea that I have some control over my thoughts was a revelation. I have gone through my life believing that I was basically stuck with my thoughts."

"I can't believe how much chatter there is in my mind. It never stops. No wonder I get headaches!"

talk is to practise *thought-stopping.*
Thought-stopping is a way of saying "NO!"
to negative or self-defeating thinking. After
all, since we are the ones who decide to play
these damaging tapes inside our heads, we are
also the ones capable of turning them off.

If it's difficult to imagine how you will
change your thoughts and beliefs
about smoking, think about a different situation where you changed
your mind. Maybe you were raised
to believe something derogatory
about women. As you became an
adult you likely started to reflect on this belief and
test it to see if it was true. After a while, you probably
saw that it was just an opinion and you had a choice
whether or not to believe it. If you made a decision
to reject it you would have said something like "No, I
don't believe that anymore." This is a form of
thought-stopping we do spontaneously. We can
make a decision to use thought-stopping in a more
conscious way to change our thinking.

"Thought-stopping helps
me. I like saying stop to
the crap. It keeps me from
spiralling down into a
depression."

Thought-stopping works like this:

Whenever you start thinking something like:
"Oh brother, I'm so stupid; everyone must think
I'm an idiot."
Say to yourself:
"STOP! I'm not stupid. So what if I made a mis-
take? I'm human like everyone else."

Whenever you start thinking something like:
"I'm so bloody angry, I could scream. If I don't
have a cigarette I'm going to blow up!"
Say to yourself:
"STOP! Okay, I know I'm angry, but smoking
won't help me. If I keep thinking it will, I'm
going to drive myself to smoke. I'll just sit here
for a couple of minutes and think this through."

Whenever you start thinking something like:

"I'm so fat. I can't believe how much cellulite I have on my thighs. I have to do something to lose this weight! Maybe I should start smoking again, until I lose this weight."

Say to yourself:

"STOP! I'm not ugly. Smoking won't help me get healthy. Thinking this way does not help me lose weight; it just makes me hate myself."

Whenever you start thinking something like:

"I'm so stressed out. There's so much going on for me. Quitting smoking is too hard. I'm going to ask my friend for a cigarette."

Say to yourself:

"STOP! There is a lot going on for me right now, but having a cigarette won't change that. This stress will pass. Quitting smoking is hard right now, but I can do it. I'll ask my friend for a hug."

"I need to realize that I am worthy. I am capable of being loved."

Thought-stopping helps us to deal with negative self-talk before it overwhelms us and damages our self-esteem. Like most new habits, we need to practise thought-stopping if we want it to work. You might find it helpful to leave little notes with positive messages around your house. These notes could say things like "I promise to be true to myself" or "I am a healthy woman. I make good choices." Notes that ask questions can help us remain mindful and encourage us to tune in to our self-talk. Examples of such questions are "Did you deep breathe today?" or "What are you thinking and feeling right now?"

"Positive self-talk just makes sense. I mean, life is tough enough. Why not talk to yourself in a kind way?"

Positive self-talk cultivates and supports high self-esteem. It is loving, accepting and encouraging. Affirmations are an example of positive self-talk. If we say, "I know I'm larger than many people think I should be but I'm healthy and strong and I'm not smoking anymore," we are participating in positive self-talk.

Positive self-talk can get us through many difficult and even painful experiences. It increases our inner resources and makes us less dependent on the advice and opinions of others. We are less vulnerable in general when we possess the ability to comfort and encourage ourselves.

Some examples of positive self-talk are:

"I know I can get through this urge. I'm a non-smoker now and I have other ways of coping with stress."

or

"I'm very angry about what that man said to me. He has no right to speak to me that way. I'm not going to let it get to me this time. I'll just give myself some time to feel angry and I'll call my friend and get some support from her too."

You will notice that when we engage in positive self-talk, we remain on our own side. This doesn't mean we can't look at ourselves critically or honestly—we just don't trash ourselves in the process.

Negative self-talk doesn't help us change. Critical, abusive chatter in our heads weakens us and makes us apathetic. When we quit smoking, we need to operate from a place of strength. Thought-stopping and positive self-talk are tools which can help us feel strong and confident.

"Smoking doesn't chase the hurts away. It just increases the hurt because I know smoking is negative."

"Changing my thinking about smoking has been powerful. I am starting to believe I can quit. This is a big deal for me!"

JOURNAL ENTRY: FREEING THE MIND

Prepare your space. Light a candle or burn incense. Start with the relaxation exercise or a few minutes of conscious breathing. Play music if you wish. When you are ready, begin writing. Ask yourself:

What ideas or thoughts need to be cleared away to prepare me for quitting smoking?

In what ways do I participate in negative and positive self-talk?

What could I start telling myself that would help me quit smoking?

Give yourself a reward when you are finished the exercise.

Freeing the Heart

Both smokers and non-smokers develop ways of expressing and repressing emotions. But for smokers, part of our way includes lighting up a cigarette. We might be so accustomed to smoking every time we feel a strong emotion that we're not sure what to do with our feelings when we don't smoke. Learning to name and express our feelings is an essential part of the quitting process. If we take the time to get in touch with the range of our feelings before we quit smoking, we are in a better position to experience them, after we quit, without wanting to smoke.

Take anger for example. We may have been taught that women should not express anger openly. We may believe that an angry woman is unfeminine or unattractive. Most women have been socialized to believe that anger is more acceptable in men than in women. We may think it's our job to comfort and soothe angry people rather than be angry. Of course, this belief doesn't keep us from *feeling* angry; it just keeps us from expressing it in healthy ways.

Smoking is one way of repressing anger. Instead

of expressing our anger or rage in a constructive way, we often light up a cigarette. When we quit, without our cigarettes to help us keep the anger in, we may become frightened of our anger. It is often out of the fear that we will explode or misdirect our anger that women start smoking again. But smoking is no guarantee that we will behave the way we think is best. Most of us have behaved in ways that we later felt badly about, even though we had our cigarettes safely in hand.

"I've never had an adult emotion without a cigarette in my hand."

Hiding our true feelings behind a "smoke screen" just makes things worse. Our bottled up emotions can make us ill. Feelings are a form of energy and need to be released. It helps to laugh. Many of us tend to take the feelings we experience when we quit smoking a little too seriously. Finding the humour in our situation can help us. We need to remember this when we are in the throes of anger or any other powerful emotion and are thinking that a cigarette would help us through. Once again, we need to return to simple, ordinary coping methods like conscious breathing and positive self-talk to get us over the hurdle.

This is not to say that we won't have a hard time with our feelings when we first quit. In fact, it is very common to experience our emotions quite intensely for several days and maybe even weeks after we quit smoking. This is partly because we may have been stifling our emotional expression by smoking but also because quitting smoking is a major change in our lives and any significant change is accompanied by strong feelings. This is especially so if we have viewed smoking as an act of nurturance or compassion toward ourselves.

We may have thought of cigarettes as a friend or companion and feel the loss in the same way we might if we ended a relationship. These feelings are real and need to be acknowledged. They are not a sign that we are weak. Talking about how we feel with people we can count on for support is probably the most effective way of working through this stage of quitting.

"Emotion is something I don't like to express for the fear that I will 'expose' myself."

In time we can learn new ways to express and honour our emotions without smoking. What's important to remember is that feelings are neither good nor bad. They simply are. If we accept that we are emotional as well as physical and intellectual beings, we won't need to escape from our emotions. We can open ourselves up to them and direct their flow in healthy ways.

FEELINGS

There are many books available which explore our emotional selves in detail. The following list offers only a brief description of the main emotions we experience.

1 Fear

Fear is vital because it alerts us to what threatens our well-being.

When we are frightened, our bodies secrete adrenaline, causing our hearts to pump rapidly, sending blood to our legs so that we react to the situation by "fighting" or "fleeing."

When we don't pay attention to and deal with our fear it can surface in other less direct ways like anxiety, paranoia and hostility.

Fear can also become ongoing worry—about our jobs, relationships, success and self-worth.

Healthy expression of fear through talking and action keeps us out of dangerous situations and helps us to distinguish between real and imaginary fears.

2   Anger

Anger alerts us to injustice and violation.

When we are angry, our bodies become tense and rigid, our hearts race and even our voices change.

When we don't pay attention to our anger, it can smoulder inside and erupt at inappropriate times, or it can surface in our body as illness.

Anger turned inward becomes depression.

Unexpressed anger causes us to become resentful and hostile toward others.

Healthy expression of anger through walking, dancing, talking or drawing, etc., helps us preserve our dignity and integrity. It prevents us from participating in back-stabbing and violence.

Part of the difficulty with anger is how we think about it. Most of us think of anger as an "action" rather than a feeling. We think anger is the same thing as yelling or hitting. An example of this is when we say "I got angry *at* him." But we don't get happy *at* someone. We *feel* angry or happy and there are many different ways to express our feelings.

"I have a hard time expressing anger constructively. I use cigarettes to suppress this anger."

3   Sadness or Grief

Sadness alerts us to a loss in our lives either of a person, thing or situation.

When we are sad we cry, lose our appetite, suffer sleep disturbances and even think differently. We may think that we are going crazy or are alone in the world or that our despair will never end.

When we resist sadness, it can surface in our bodies as illness, in our lives as workaholism or as a continued but false expression of cheerfulness.

Healthy expression of sadness through crying, talking, writing, etc., allows us to recognize loss in our lives, opens our hearts to other emotions and deepens our experience of love and life.

4 Joy

Joy is an expression of well-being and connection to other living beings and the earth. We experience joy when we are in touch with our own divinity and that of others.

When we are joyful, our skin glows, we look healthier and we move our bodies with greater ease and grace.

We experience joy when we allow our other emotions to flow freely. We sabotage our experience of joy when we believe too much of a good thing is bad or when we expect the worst in situations so we won't be disappointed.

Joy is expressed through song, dance, touch, laughing, talking, sex, etc.

Joy expands our ability to love and accept others and keeps us in touch with the wonder and beauty of life.

"It wasn't just anger that was a problem. I had a hard time showing my joy. I felt guilty feeling happy when so many of my friends were down. Imagine that! Quitting for me meant doing what I needed to be whole. I'm really happy that I don't smoke and I'm letting it show!"

COPING WITH STRESS

One of the main reasons smokers say they have a difficult time quitting and staying off cigarettes is *stress*. Since stress appears to be on the increase in our society, it's worth taking some time to understand what it is.

Even though stress has been around since time began, most people did not use this word until the late 1950s. It was at this time that Dr. Hans Selye was conducting research on what happens when animals are injured or placed in unusual or extreme conditions. Dr. Selye said, "Stress is the nonspecific response of the organism to any pressure or demand." In other words, *the event or situation is the stressor and our response is the stress.*

"I never feel sure of what I really feel. If I say something I'm afraid I'll change my mind and seem wishy-washy. But I like to look at every angle and put myself in each situation and into the other person's place."

To make things even more interesting, Dr. Selye discovered that a stressor can be an internal or external event. For example, our thoughts can be the cause of our stress. If we continually engage in negative self-talk we start to feel very stressed.

Not everyone will experience stress over the same event. Each of us filters what we see through our own personal lens. How stressed out we get depends on factors such as our coping skills, our self-esteem, our personal values and our sense of humour. A flat tire might spell disaster for the woman who doesn't know how to fix it and has no money to pay for someone else to do it. For another woman who has been taught how to repair flats, it might be a minor annoyance.

Dr. Selye said that animals and people tend to respond to a stressor by either *fleeing* the situation or *fighting*. Our bodies release biochemicals that make this possible. Adrenaline, for example, makes our hearts beat faster in an effort to pump more blood to the muscles that need it. Unfortunately, many of us find ourselves in stressful situations where it's not appropriate to flee or fight. The stress hormones we release during these situations can damage our immune systems and cause illness over time.

There are countless other examples of how our modern society creates situations—crime, violence, economic insecurity and environmental devastation—which contribute to our feelings of being overwhelmed by stress. In spite of this, it is possible to find ways of coping instead of feeling constantly stressed out.

"I can cope with my feelings without being overwhelmed."

Dr. Selye noticed that both people and animals went through changes to cope with the stressor. He called the ability to change in order to deal with a situation *adaptability*. Adaptability can be both positive and negative. For example, using positive self-talk to cope with the fear and nervousness we might feel returning to school as mature students makes us stronger. It is a positive way of adapting to a stressful situation. On the other hand, trying to adapt to living in an abusive relationship or nasty work environment can harm us. These are the situations that need to change or we need to leave in order to stay well.

Smoking is an interesting example of negative adaptation for two reasons. First of all, we use smoking as a way of adapting or dealing with stress although, as we have discussed, nicotine actually stimulates, rather than relaxes, our nervous systems. Second, when we first started smoking, our bodies reacted strongly to the poisons in the cigarettes (unless we had been exposed to smoking throughout our childhood) by coughing, feeling dizzy and even throwing up. When we continued to smoke, our bodies began to adapt and stopped sending us messages to quit. But adapting to smoking weakens our bodies and eventually causes illness and death. It is a serious example of negative adaptation.

Dealing with stress in positive ways begins with developing a realistic sense of what we have control over. Many women have found the Serenity Prayer from Alcoholics Anonymous helpful in maintaining a healthy perspective on life. If the idea of "God" doesn't fit with your view of life, replace it with another concept or word that expresses your values. Some women find this prayer has more meaning if they say "Goddess" or "Creative Universe" or "Great Spirit" or "Creator." Do what works for you.

> "The alternative to expressing my feelings is stuffing them and that was making me sick. I don't want to smoke, eat or drink my feelings away anymore. I want to feel them and that's just what I'm doing!"

> God grant me the serenity
> to accept the things
> I cannot change
> The courage to change
> the things I can
> And the wisdom
> to know the difference.

Taking time for ourselves, resting, using positive self-talk and exercising are other effective ways of coping with stress. Sometimes just going for a walk can make a big difference. Pay attention to how your body feels in a stressful situation. Where do you hold the tension? Use conscious breathing and relaxation to release stress. Quieting our minds helps us know what we might have to change in our lives. Perhaps we need to confront a situation or leave a job. Whatever it is, smoking won't make it better. In tough moments, instead of lighting up, remind yourself that "this, too, shall pass."

WAYS TO HELP YOU EXPRESS FEELINGS

Check-ins

One way of understanding and expressing our feelings is to check in with ourselves several times daily. The best times are usually morning and evening since these are transition times during our day. When we check in, we ask ourselves these three questions:

I feel _____

I need _____

I want _____

Check-ins help us to label our emotions accurately and encourage us to take action.

Affirmations

Affirmations can help us to accept ourselves as emotional beings. They can encourage us to trust in our ability to express our feelings in ways that enhance our well-being. (Look back to the section on affirmations in Chapter 2 to develop your affirmations.) Try developing affirmations such as "I express my anger in respectful ways" or "I am in touch with my feelings."

Constructive Criticism

We can engage in healthy conflict if we remember to keep the other person's feelings in mind and use statements that begin with *I* instead of *you. You* statements put the other person on the defensive. Also, we should try not to name-call when we are expressing our anger.

"I've had to learn how to say how I feel and what I want. It gets easier all the time."

This formula for constructive criticism can be helpful: I feel (*describe your feeling*) when you (*describe their behaviour*). I would feel better if you would (*propose an alternative*).

Creative Emotional Release

There are many wonderful and creative ways to release our feelings. Don't limit yourself to only one or two ways. Sometimes it is more helpful to rent a sad movie and have a good cry than it is to call your mother to tell her she drives you crazy. Sometimes we can't explain why we're sad—we just are. Other times we don't want to talk about our feelings, or maybe we're bored with them. In these situations, creating a piece of art or gardening would be a more positive release. Women in

Catching Our Breath groups have also found the following effective ways of releasing and transforming strong feelings:

Painting
Going for a drive
Massage
Rocking in a rocking chair
Walking
Making love or self-pleasuring
Listening to music
Cleaning
Telling silly, ridiculous, raunchy jokes
Throwing stuff out
Making delicious food
Building something
Dancing
Getting a tattoo

JOURNAL ENTRY: FREEING THE HEART

Prepare your space. Light a candle or burn incense.
Begin with the relaxation exercise or a few minutes of
conscious breathing. When you are ready, start writing.
Ask yourself:

What emotions are the most difficult for me to express?

*How have I used smoking to express or repress my
emotions?*

What are my fears about quitting smoking? Develop an affirmation that counters this fear.

Also create a statement about smoking and letting go, something like:

In the past I used cigarettes to help me deal with my feelings of _____

I now express this directly by _____

_____

Give yourself a reward when you are finished the exercise.

Freeing the Body

Remember how we felt after our first cigarette? Even though we may not experience the same immediate negative response to smoking now, we know that smoking is hurting us. Eventually we need to pay attention to this truth or, as writer Alice Miller says, "The body will present its bill."

Quitting smoking can be an especially empowering experience for women because it helps to restore respect and love for our bodies. As women, we have suffered many violations to our bodies in the form of sexual and physical abuse, invasive and dangerous medical interventions, sexual harassment, pornography and weight-control methods. It's no wonder that many of us have learned to mistrust or ignore any messages from our bodies and generally view our bodies with contempt and disgust. Although this may sound like an exaggerated view of how women feel about their bodies, we have only to look at the number of women driven to diet clinics and plastic surgeons (which are only two of many examples) to see sweeping self-loathing.

Because body image is a such a difficult issue for most women in this culture, it is important to address it when trying to quit smoking. If we don't, we are more likely to fall into the trap of worrying about our weight rather than caring for our health. Some doctors say that a woman would have to gain at least 100 pounds to create a health risk that equals smoking. Other researchers say that no matter what our weight gain, smoking is always more hazardous to our health. Researchers have also found that when we compare the weights of a group of non-smokers to a group of smokers, the non-smokers weigh on average only five pounds more. And not all quitters gain weight. Those who do normally lose it once they become comfortable as non-smokers.

Instead of trying to conform to unrealistic expectations of what our bodies should look like, we can expand our idea of what is acceptable and beautiful. In fact, we have only to look back about 40 years to see that even within the fashion industry, women who were considered attractive were bigger than is now the fashion. If we want to go back even farther in history, we see ancient cultures that

"Thank goodness weight control never entered my mind as a reason to smoke. I worry about the young girls now and how they smoke to stay skinny. There's too much pressure on us women to look a certain way."

worshipped a female divinity who was portrayed with large breasts, belly and thighs.

We can also look to different contemporary cultures who have not lost touch with their goddess-worshipping roots. Many women of colour have written about their experience of being large as powerful and positive. There are many examples of voluptuous goddesses from cultures all over the world (see *Goddess Remembered*, a National Film Board production).

In our own lives, we can think about who we consider attractive. Often these will be women who vary greatly from the current ideals of beauty. Their bodies may show the natural effects of child-bearing and age—full hips, round belly, sagging breasts. They may be strong women who look as if they enjoy life and feel comfortable in their own bodies. This can be one of the most appealing qualities in a woman. Acknowledging this, we can start looking at the possibility that we carry a double standard—appreciating (or at least accepting) in other women what we despise in ourselves. Perhaps then we can start being gentler with ourselves.

Size isn't the only obstruction to experiencing a positive body image. If we are differently abled in any way or do not fit the concept of what a woman should look like because we can't walk or move freely, we can also suffer from self-loathing. When we expand our ideas about how large we can be, we also need to include every woman's appearance as acceptable. No matter who we are, each of us is capable of finding beauty in ourselves.

"It's weird, but I got a lot more hassle for being a large woman than I did for smoking. I've quit now and I feel great .. I'm trying to love my body more now too."

EXERCISE

Participating in some form of movement that you enjoy is a sure way of connecting with your body and improving your body image. Our bodies are supposed to move. Our muscles, bones, internal organs and everything else you can think of that's inside of us gets healthier and stronger when we exercise. Thousands of studies have proven that exercise reduces our risk of numerous diseases (including heart disease, for which many smokers are at risk), improves our mental health, slows down the aging process and keeps our brains healthy.

In previous chapters we mentioned that smoking helps trigger endorphins, which are the "feel good" hormones, and that smoking also serves as a mental prompt to help us shift into the pleasant-feeling alpha and theta brain wave patterns. We said that there were healthier alternatives. We've already discussed how relaxation and visualization are two. Exercise is the other potent alternative. It is more effective than smoking (and certainly healthier) at releasing brain chemicals, such as endorphins and enkephalins, that increase our overall sense of well-being.

"I am slowly learning to appreciate my body, the stability, the freedom of movement."

Exercise is such a significant factor in helping women quit smoking that women in Catching Our Breath groups are encouraged to start some form of exercise early in the program. By the time women set a date to quit smoking, they have been walking, doing aerobics or engaging in some other form of exercise for at least four weeks. Although a few weeks of exercise doesn't turn us into athletes, it does ease the transition from smoker to non-smoker. Exercise can ease withdrawal and recovery symptoms because moving our bodies facilitates healing. The two organs in our bodies most damaged by smoking—our hearts and lungs—are strengthened by exercise.

Our circulation, which is also compromised by smoking, improves too.

As well, our fears about coping with stress and strong emotions after we quit are reduced because we have experienced the benefits of exercise in dealing with both.

The benefits of exercise are so amazing it's worth exploring the subject further. A list of books on the topic is included at the end of the journal. The exercise most favoured by women in Catching Our Breath groups is walking. Here are some tips to get you started.

Walking Tips

1 Wear comfortable running shoes and loose clothing.
2 Start with a few warm-up stretches and end with a few cool-down stretches.
3 Bring water with you and sip it along the way. It's really important not to get dehydrated.
4 Walk briskly, but don't push yourself. You should be able to carry on a conversation. Stop if you feel any pain.
5 Breathe!
6 Try using the time to repeat your affirmation in rhythm with your footsteps or listen to your favourite music. Make the walk fun and positive.
7 Try walking briskly for 20 minutes every day.
8 Swinging your arms will create a massaging action on the lymph glands in your armpits and stimulate the natural detoxifying function of these glands.
9 Find a friend who can be a walking buddy. Having a friend to walk with increases our chances of sticking to a program during tough times and in cold weather.

10　If it gets so cold outside that even walking with a friend and talking doesn't help, try walking at an indoor track. Most YWCAs have indoor tracks.

11　If you have small children, include them in your walks by pushing them in a stroller. Even "bigger" kids get a thrill out of riding in a stroller. It's a great way of diffusing parent/child stress, and think of what a positive fitness example you're setting for your family!

If you are not able to walk, or if walking is just not your "thing," try something else that gets you moving and raises your heart rate. Some ideas include:

1　Dance

Put on your favourite music and just let go in your living room or join a class.

2　Aerobics

Classes are offered almost everywhere or you can rent (or buy) exercise videos from your video store. Try any of Susan Powter's or Kathy Smith's. Jane Fonda's *Step and Stretch* is a favourite. If possible, preview a video before you buy it. There are many bad exercise videos on the market.

3　Yoga

There are several types of yoga. This physical discipline is becoming so popular that many community and fitness centres now offer classes. It's excellent for increasing strength and flexibility. The magazine *Yoga Journal* is available at many libraries and is a helpful resource for learning more about yoga and yoga-related books and videos. B.S. Iyengar's book *Light on Yoga* is a classic and is also very helpful for beginners.

4   Weight Training

Using three- to five-pound hand weights a few times each week converts fat into muscle, builds our strength, increases bone density and tones our bodies. Muscle tissue has a higher "metabolic" rate than fat, which means it uses more energy, so the more muscle we have the more calories we burn. This might be of special interest to smokers who are worried about a decrease in their metabolic rate after quitting. Most fitness experts now recommend that we include weight training in addition to aerobic exercise. Susan Powter's *Building Strength* video is excellent for women of all sizes and fitness levels.

5   Swimming

Swimming is a great exercise to ease the stiffness and back pain of lower-back problems and arthritis. And it can help us prevent injuries to our joints and bones. Being immersed in water can be especially appealing when we are experiencing recovery symptoms after we quit smoking.

Obviously, these are just a few of the many possibilities for exercise and fitness. You might want to speak with a fitness consultant to develop your own exercise program. Be creative and have fun!

As authors Regina Sara Ryan and John W. Travis say in their book *Wellness: Small Changes You Can Use to Make a Big Difference*:

> You know yourself which exercise form you are more likely to stay with. Avoid setting yourself up for failure and disappointment by forcing yourself to be brave or strong about your exercise. Taking a vigorous walk around your block every day is infinitely more beneficial than dreaming about doing a triathlon.

STRETCHING

Here are some easy stretches to do to increase your flexibility and general vitality. Another way to enhance your energy is to simply make your daily activities more active. Take the stairs instead of the elevator, walk to work, plan a walk every morning or at lunch, spend some of your visiting times with your friends walking instead of sitting and talking.

1   Shoulder Stretch

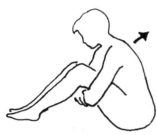

Sit on floor, legs extended.

Bend legs, clasping arms under knees. Hug knees to chest.

Gently pull torso away from knees, while continuing to clasp arms.

Breathe. Hold for a few seconds and repeat.

2   Shoulder and Back "Massage"

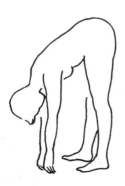

Stand firmly grounded, feet shoulder-width apart.

Raise arms over head, elbows slightly bent.

With knees slightly bent, slowly bend forward from hips.

Relax upper body. Breathe. Let everything dangle: head, neck and arms.

Slowly straighten up, vertebra by vertebra, starting from bottom of spine.

3 Child's Pose

Sit back on heels.

Slowly bend until torso rests on knees.

Nestle yourself into a comfortable
position.

Rest arms by your sides. Breathe.

Release neck, shoulders and back.

Breathe. Hold as long as you wish.

4 Waist Stretch

Stand firmly grounded, legs about three feet
apart.

Bend right knee; rest arm on thigh.

Raise other arm, shifting weight to the
right.

Reach over head until you feel a gentle
stretch along the waist.

Hold a few seconds and repeat on the
other side.

MASSAGE

Massage has tremendous healing powers. Massage
can hasten our recovery from smoking as well as
increase our pleasure and energy. If you have someone with whom you can share massage, try to fit one
session of massage into each week. It's a wonderful
way of nurturing a friendship and feeling close without talking. Massage is something you can enjoy by
yourself as well. Treat massage like you would your
relaxation or writing exercise.

"I spent most of my life
feeling disconnected
from my body. It was kind
of just 'there.' Stopping
smoking has helped me
pay attention to it and
learn what a wonderful
gift it is to have a body."

Prepare a space; light a candle.

Play relaxing music.

Using pleasant-smelling oil or lotion, begin working on your feet with slow, firm strokes. Move to your calves and thighs.

Massage your hands, arms and neck. Remember to take slow, deep breaths.

It's also relaxing to massage your face and scalp. We hold a lot of tension in our heads, which can cause headaches and migraines. Massage can help release this tension and reduce our need for pain medication.

Experiment with massage! Do what feels right for you!

BREATHING

We have already discussed the importance of conscious breathing in Chapter 2. Breathing is what keeps us alive. Smoking threatens our ability to breathe more than anything else does. Even before we quit smoking we should practise breathing fully and deeply. After we quit, deep breathing is amazingly helpful in getting us through smoking urges. Look back to Chapter 2 for the simple breathing exercise, or you can try this variation of deep breathing when you get a strong urge to smoke.

Form your mouth into a little circle and draw in air like you would drag on a cigarette. Let your head fall back.

Hold for a moment.

Now blow out like you would exhale smoke, bringing your head forward.

REST

A recent study showed that people today get, on average, two hours less sleep every night than did our ancestors. Over time this lack of sleep adds up, creating a significant sleep deficit in our lives, which can damage our immune systems and reduce our ability to function.

In the U.S. over 500 million visits to the doctor each year are about fatigue. In one study 28% of women said fatigue was a major problem in their lives. There are many causes of fatigue, including viruses, depression, sleep disorders, environmental toxins, sex hormones, thyroid problems and poor diet (Hoffman 1993).

Many women have their sleep interrupted because of pregnancy and caring for children. As well, women who were abused as children (or adults) may find that they do not feel safe enough to relax at night. These problems are increased if we are under stress or living in noisy or crowded conditions.

As smokers, we may turn to our cigarettes (and coffee) to keep us awake or to deal with sleeplessness. These stimulants just make things worse because they interfere with the quality of our sleep and set a vicious cycle in motion: the more tired we are, the more we rely on substances to keep us awake, which in turn makes it difficult to sleep, making us even more tired in the morning.

Our success in staying off cigarettes increases if we take the time to examine the quality of our sleep and how rested we feel. For some women this might mean a visit to the doctor to find out if there are medical reasons for our fatigue. Most of us will be able to improve our sleep quality by learning relaxation techniques, exercising and changing our diet.

The importance of rest cannot be overstated. Restful sleep gives us more energy, improves our mental and emotional functioning and increases our optimism about life. The following are some suggestions for getting a better night's sleep (adapted from Spangler 1996).

1   Make your bedroom a restful place:
Buy cotton or flannel sheets. Get a good mattress or foamies and pillow. Clean out the clutter and junk. Keep your room clean and organized. Position your bed so that you can see the door, and remove anything from the wall over your bed that could fall on your head. Put something beautiful by your bedside, such as flowers or a picture of someone you love. Choose curtains that you really like, and make sure that they keep out the light and provide privacy.

2   Slow down before bedtime:
Try not to smoke or drink caffeine in the evening. Drink chamomile or peppermint tea instead. Don't watch upsetting television programs or read books that agitate you. Try listening to soothing music. Place a sachet of lavender under your pillow.

3   Make a safe nest:
Install both smoke and carbon monoxide detectors near each bedroom in your home. Put a lock on your bedroom door if you worry that someone may come in uninvited and disrupt your sleep. Put a "Do Not Disturb" sign on your door.

4   Have a light in the darkness:
If you tend to get up at night to go to the bathroom, buy yourself a night light for your bathroom and hallway.

5   Breathe:
Spend a few moments deep breathing once you are in bed. Sleep with your window opened just a crack to get fresh air. Put a fern or a spider plant in your bedroom to help purify the air.

WAYS TO WAKE UP AND
INVIGORATE THE BODY

Some people have observed that smoking is a misguided attempt to invigorate and wake up the body.
There are healthier alternatives.

Sight

No matter how modest our homes or workplaces
are, we can still bring visual beauty into them. Try
adding plants, photographs, a brightly coloured scarf
or piece of fabric, or whatever you enjoy looking at.

Sound

Check your list of sounds from Chapter 2 and make
a conscious effort to bring these sounds into your
life.

Smell

Use perfumes, herbs, oils, incense, flowers and the
smell of cooking to awaken your sense of smell.
Learn more about aromatherapy and its ability to
improve our concentration, help us to relax and lift
our moods.

Touch

Instead of cigarettes, try holding small smooth
stones, crystals or other small objects. Apply hand
lotion a few times each day.

Taste

Our sense of taste does improve after we quit smoking. One way to help our taste buds is to use a natural toothpaste and mouthwash. These products are
sugar-free and contain herbs that clean our gums
and tongues as well as our teeth. Brushing our
tongues will remove the coating caused by smoking.

WAYS TO CREATE A POSITIVE BODY IMAGE

"I spend way more time on self-care now. Just little things, like bath oil, hand lotion, nice underwear and regular haircuts have really improved my self-esteem."

"Was I ever happy with my body? I think I was when I was young before puberty, when I wasn't self-conscious. My body was efficient and light. I ran easily and had lots of energy."

1. Wear clothing that fits comfortably and feels good on the skin. Don't try to fit into clothing that is too small.

2. Wear shoes that support the feet and allow you to break into a run or dance at will. Most of us need to increase our shoe size as we get older or gain weight.

3. Create affirmations that encourage you to love and accept your body right now. You could try "My body is healthy and strong" or "I love and approve of my body right now."

4. Practise thought-stopping techniques whenever you begin to insult yourself. Remember that hating your body won't help you to change it. Insults demoralize us and can cause us to overeat or abuse ourselves.

5. If people make critical comments about your body, tell them how it makes you feel and ask them to stop. Nobody has the right to put down another person's appearance.

6   Remove yourself from situations and people that make you feel badly about your body or appearance.

7   Turn your bathing times into self-care rituals. Use shampoos, bubble baths or lotions that you really like. Light a candle.

8   No matter what your size or fitness level, find a daily physical exercise that you can do and enjoy. Try yoga, walking, cycling or low-impact aerobics.

9   Don't postpone haircuts, buying clothes, learning new things or whatever it is you want to do, until you lose weight. Live life now!

HEALTHY WAYS TO FEED THE BODY

1   Learn to tune in to your hunger signals. Eat when you're hungry but try not to skip meals.

2   Eat lots of vegetables, fruits and grains high in fibre.

3   Replenish your body with the vitamin C that was depleted by smoking. Broccoli and cantaloupe are good sources. Speak to a nutritionist or other health practitioner about vitamin and mineral supplements. Consider taking a vitamin B complex, calcium, magnesium and vitamin C.

4   Drink at least eight glasses of water each day.

5   Try to avoid junk food but don't abuse yourself if you do indulge. Allowing ourselves occasional "bad foods" can keep us from binging on them out of a sense of deprivation.

6   If you are struggling with an eating disorder, such as starving yourself or throwing up to lose weight, find a counsellor and get help. You are not alone.

JOURNAL ENTRY: FREEING THE BODY

Prepare your space. Light a candle or burn incense.
Begin with the relaxation exercise or a few minutes of
conscious breathing. When you are ready, start writing.
Ask yourself:

Was there a time when I was happy with my body?

How was my life different then?

If you can't think of a time when you liked your body, try to imagine what your life would be like if the female body was honoured in all its shapes and sizes.

What keeps you from experiencing those feelings now?

How does smoking fit with how you feel about your body?

List some ways you can improve your body image.

Give yourself a reward when you are finished the exercise.

Bringing It All Together and Quitting

So far, we've been exploring many of the reasons why we smoke. We know we're not stupid for smoking, nor are we hopeless addicts. We smoke out of a desire to soothe and comfort ourselves as well as to meet other legitimate needs. Our belief that "smoking makes it better" keeps us turning to our cigarettes to feel centred.

But we also know that smoking doesn't really meet any of these needs. Eventually we need to let go of our cigarettes and create new ways of giving ourselves the things we've been seeking through smoking. We've discussed how cultivating mindfulness, changing our self-talk, doing relaxation exercises, practising affirmations, writing, dancing, walking, exercising, eating well, resting and doing the things we love are ways we can get unhooked. Now it's time to gather that knowledge together, look honestly at how smoking hurts us and make a change!

At this point, it's very common to feel as if there are two of us. One is ready to confront the dangers of smoking and say good-bye to cigarettes forever.

The other is worried about being able to live without cigarettes and very sad about leaving behind the dependable friend that cigarettes might have become. It's normal to feel this way. Our hesitation or apprehension about quitting does not mean that we're not ready to quit. In fact, it's a healthy sign that shows we understand the importance of the step we're about to take.

Quitting smoking represents a big change in our lives. Any significant change is accompanied by at least some doubt and concern. It's important to acknowledge our fears without letting them overwhelm us. At some point, most changes require us to set our worries aside and take the leap, even though we're not absolutely sure where we'll land.

The wonderful thing about trying to quit smoking is that no matter how we do—whether we quit for a few hours, a day, a week or a few months—we are always better off for having done it. We have given our bodies a reprieve from all the poisons in cigarettes, and we have practised being non-smokers. And as we discussed earlier, each attempt at quitting increases our chances of success.

Timing is important. What might seem like a good time to quit for one woman could seem like the worst time to someone else. Only you know whether or not the time is right. It's a good idea to think about what day is best beforehand, so that you can visualize what might happen on that day and how you can handle difficult situations. Obviously, it's a good idea to avoid days which you know are going to be stressful.

Pay attention to where you are in your menstrual cycle. Quitting during your premenstrual time—especially if you suffer from PMS—is not a good idea. We tend to experience our feelings and stress

"When I finally quit for good it was because I stopped believing in the cigarette and its power to comfort me. Slowly I started to believe in the power of me."

more deeply during this time. It might be better to set your quitting day for the first day of your period. Some women see menstruation as a time of renewal and feel quitting fits in nicely with this. Other women say the "No more bullshit!" attitude they feel during their premenstrual time fuelled their determination to quit smoking. If you can't think of a good day to quit, then choose a day that has some positive significance (e.g., International Women's Day) to remind you of how positive your decision to quit smoking is, no matter how tough the day.

Preparing ourselves for some of the emotional changes we will experience when we quit is another way of easing the transition into our lives as non-smokers. Quitting smoking is almost always perceived as a loss by smokers. It might help to know that there are identifiable feelings associated with loss.

It is common to first experience some form of *confusion* or *denial*. We might hear ourselves saying something like "Maybe I don't really need to quit smoking now. I don't think I'm doing that much damage to myself. Besides, what about all the pollution out there? That's pretty dangerous too!" Another form of denial is when we don't acknowledge our difficulties. We might say, "Quitting is a breeze. I know I won't have any trouble staying off cigarettes!" Not everyone will experience confusion or denial in these ways. Some women say they simply feel numb.

The next feelings we may experience are *anger* and *depression*. Many women feel mad at the world for having to give up something that brings them pleasure. Other women say that they are just plain mad and can't explain why. Sometimes our anger turns into depression. We may feel that we are being deprived of something. Or we might feel that no one really understands what we are going through. It's very common to want to just sit down and cry. All of this is normal.

"I'm determined to live by my values, so I'm quitting."

"I'm sick of the smell, the cost, the whole mess that smoking is!"

"I can't believe how much I cried when I quit smoking. I was really worried I was going to lapse into a terrible depression. I needed to see my therapist more frequently for a while. I'm so glad I didn't panic and start smoking again out of fear. It took a few weeks to start feeling better. I can honestly say I won't go back to smoking."

"It's true going through withdrawal will be tough for a while—but only for a while."

Eventually, if we hang in there, we will begin to feel more centred about not smoking. This is the *acceptance stage*. Our anger and sadness subside, and we sense a growing feeling of peace and pride over quitting. Of course, these feelings do not occur in the same order for everyone. And not everyone will necessarily experience all the feelings. Many of us will be extremely happy about our decision to quit for a few days and then become very sad or angry. Some of us won't experience much grief at all. There is no way to know for sure what we will feel. It's best to be prepared for the full range of feelings and allow ourselves to express them openly.

We can help ourselves move through these emotional changes by first acknowledging our feelings, rather than denying they exist. Whatever our experience, it will always be helpful to express our most intense feelings through talking, writing and moving our bodies.

"Before I became pregnant I quit smoking. It was exciting for me because I was preparing my body and I knew I was really going to get pregnant!"

Just as we cannot predict exactly how we will feel when we quit, there is also no way to predict which women will have a more difficult time quitting. We might think a woman who has smoked heavily for many years will experience the toughest time. In fact, she might be so determined to get cigarettes out of her life that her quitting flows more easily than for the light smoker who approaches quitting only half-heartedly. The *strength of our desire to quit and our belief that we can do it* are really the most important factors in determining our success.

"Smoking has been my anchor. It's not easy finding a new one, but it's worth it."

Take a look at your Smoker's Wheel of Change and think about what you have written. What areas of your wheel are weak? What do you need to do to strengthen these? Remember the importance of support. If it's possible, tell a friend about your decision to quit smoking. A supportive friend can listen to us during the times we need to talk, validate our feelings, give us encouragement, and believe in us when we doubt our ability to quit. It's important to choose someone who's not going to stomp all over you if you do slip and have a couple of cigarettes. You need to be able to admit you smoked without feeling guilt or shame. Talking about relapse with someone can help you work through your reasons for your slip and keep you from abandoning your efforts to quit.

If you feel you just are not ready to quit smoking, don't be discouraged. Quitting smoking is *your* decision and you need to do it in your own way. As we discussed in the chapter on Change, each of us goes through several stages before we are ready to take action. It could be that you are still in the preparation stage and need to become more skilled in new coping methods before you give up smoking. Or you need to further develop your reasons for quitting. Maybe you don't feel ready to cope with the discomfort of not smoking. Whatever your reasons, try not to completely abandon the idea of quitting *at some point*. In the meantime, there are other smaller changes you can make.

You might want to try reducing the amount you smoke or changing the places where you smoke. The following list of changes will help you become more skilled at being a non-smoker and build your confidence to quit smoking. Reducing the amount we smoke is only a short-term measure.

Smoking even a few cigarettes each day still damages our health. And sometimes small changes are harder to maintain than big changes because we experience "the worst of both worlds." No matter how much we cut down, we never get rid of our craving for cigarettes and we don't benefit from the larger health and self-esteem rewards that come from quitting. If we want to be free of our addiction and improve our health, eventually we need to completely quit smoking.

"I've tried so many times to quit and I'm still trying. But I don't want my kids exposed to the poisons that I am, so I smoke outside now."

TIPS FOR CUTTING DOWN

1   Eliminate the cigarettes that you smoke "automatically," just because they are handy. Review Chapter 5 on Awareness.

2   Attach your own message to your cigarette package, one that encourages you to breathe and think a few minutes before you light up. It could say something like "Take a deep breath. What do you really want?"

3   Use positive self-talk to practise saying no to some of your smoking urges. You could say something like "I really want a cigarette, but I'm going to breathe for a few minutes and see what happens to this craving. If I want, I can have a smoke in 15 minutes."

4   Switch to a brand of cigarettes which is lower in tar and nicotine than the brand you usually smoke.

"Massage has been my stress reliever. It has made a huge difference in reducing my cravings."

5   When you go out, only take the number of cigarettes you want to smoke and avoid asking for more if you smoke them all.

6   Choose the times of the day that you could eliminate smoking. For example, you could postpone your morning cigarette until 9 a.m. on weekdays and until noon on weekends. Or you could decide that you won't smoke after 10 p.m.

7   Sit in no-smoking sections of restaurants.

8   Avoid smoking around children.

9   Make your house a smoke-free zone or limit smoking to one room only. Smoke outside instead.

10   Practise "quitting" for a few hours or a day each week. Try to extend the time you go smoke-free each week.

11   Count the number of cigarettes you did *not* smoke. For example, if you usually smoke 25 cigarettes each day and you cut out the first and last cigarettes of the day, eliminate two cigarettes

that you "automatically" light up, and postpone one cigarette by breathing through a tough urge, you will have not smoked five cigarettes. That's 35 cigarettes or a pack and a half in one week!

12 Visualize yourself as a non-smoker. Review Chapter 2 on Practices. *Practise, practise, practise!*

The next few pages outline more practical tips for quitting and coping. Research has shown that successful quitters make use of a combination of methods. *Catching Our Breath* is based on natural, simple and ordinary methods that don't cost money. Research and our own experience have taught us that practices such as conscious breathing, relaxation, positive self-talk and exercise *are effective*. However, you may want to try other aids such as the nicotine patch. Some women have found the patch helpful, while others say it was expensive and ineffective. It's very important *not* to smoke and use the patch at the same time. Nicotine is an extremely potent drug that can kill us. After all, isn't that why we're trying to quit smoking? Talk to your physician for more information. Even if you don't want the patch or nicotine gum, let her know that you are quitting smoking. A good doctor will be thrilled with the news and will lend support and encouragement.

> "One of my triumphs was going through the check-out at the grocery store and feeling so happy that I didn't even want to buy a package of smokes!"

Don't waste your time looking for "magical solutions" or shifting your reliance from the cigarette to another crutch. Quitting smoking is about depending on ourselves. Methods such as acupuncture and the patch are most effective if they are combined with the coping methods we've been discussing. In the end it will take commitment and practice to overcome your addiction.

> "I don't take my quitting for granted. Every day I'm careful. I pay attention to my needs because I know for me it would be easy to slip back into my old habits."

Quitting smoking is one of the most important decisions you can make because it can save your life. Quitting will mean putting your needs first for a while. You have to believe you are worth it. Remember, everything you need to know about quitting is contained within you. You were not born smoking. Your body will remember how to live without cigarettes. Trust in your wisdom and you will become a non-smoker!

ALTERNATIVE TREATMENTS THAT CAN HELP US

"I've starting using aromatherapy since I quit smoking. I love it. My home smells so beautiful and when I'm at work I have a little spritzer I spray around my desk that is a real pick-me-up. I don't know how I ever stomached the smell of cigarettes."

More and more women are turning to alternative methods of treating addictions. Alternative methods include both new and traditional ways of helping the body heal (Baar 1994). Because of the consumer demand for alternatives to drugs and surgery, many physicians who practise conventional medicine are learning about these therapies and are beginning to work with the health practitioners who use them. Choosing an alternative health practitioner is similar to choosing a doctor. A recommendation from a friend is probably the most common way of finding a practitioner. It's essential that you feel comfortable with the practitioner and that you stay away from therapies that don't make sense to you, despite how highly recommended they might come. The following is a sampling of alternative treatments that women in Catching Our Breath groups have found helpful in quitting smoking.

Acupuncture

"In my culture, it's the men that smoke. That was part of the lure for me starting to smoke."

This involves the insertion of fine sterile needles into the body at points along the meridians through which the *chi*, or vital energy, is said to flow. The needles help to restore the normal flow of this energy. Acupuncture has been used to reduce or eliminate cravings for tobacco and has helped speed up the recovery process.

Ayurveda

Ayurveda operates on the principle that each person has a unique constitution determined by individual physical, emotional, spiritual and mental traits called *doshas*. The goal of Ayurvedic medicine is to keep your life force free-flowing by keeping your constitution in balance. A practitioner might recommend a blend of diet, sleep, work and other habits specifically tailored to your constitution. Dr. Deepak Chopra's book *Perfect Health* is a helpful guide on this subject.

"Because I was raised in a very religious family I thought smoking was a good way to rebel. I really didn't want to be uptight and judgmental like my relatives. I have to work at not associating smoking with freedom, because that's what I thought it was when I was a kid."

Bodywork

This general category includes hands-on therapies designed to stimulate the nervous and lymphatic systems, to stretch and relax muscles, and to improve circulation. Women who are quitting smoking find massage extremely beneficial in dealing with recovery symptoms and releasing tension. Bodywork of all kinds is a favoured healing method of women in Catching Our Breath groups.

"I only started to smoke when I was a university student in Canada. Smoking kind of went with my learning to speak English and fit into this culture."

Homeopathy

This is a system based on the "Law of Similars," which means that the same substance that causes particular symptoms in a healthy person will, when given in extremely small doses, cure a sick person who exhibits those same symptoms. Homeopaths take a detailed history and prescribe a specific remedy. Many homeopathic medicines are considered over-the-counter drugs and are available at health food stores. There are a few specifically for smokers trying to quit.

"I shared my first cigarette when I came out as a lesbian to a friend at school. She was a smoker and was so overwhelmed by my 'confession' that she lit up a cigarette and handed me one. I remember she said, 'If you're a lesbian then being a lesbian must be a good thing.' I think after that I connected smoking to trust and intimacy and self-approval. I think that's why quitting has felt so hard—like I was giving up all that comfort and safety."

Naturopathy

Sometimes naturopaths are called the general practitioners of natural medicine because they draw from many systems of alternative medicine. Naturopaths take a detailed medical history and may suggest any number of treatments, including rest, dietary changes, vitamins and minerals, homeopathy or acupuncture. Naturopaths stress non-invasive treatments that stimulate the body's natural healing power. Women trying to quit are often encouraged to change their diet, get more rest and take certain vitamin and mineral supplements.

THE EFFECTS OF SMOKING ON OUR BODIES

Smoking is often more serious a health risk than we know. Smoking kills more people than heroin, cocaine, alcohol, AIDS, fires, homicide, suicide and automobile accidents combined. Although it is hard to look honestly at the harmful effects of smoking, we need to open ourselves up to the truth about cigarettes if we are going to let go of them for good. Take some time to sit quietly and focus on facts such as these.

Each year in Canada, at least 13,000 women die a tobacco-related death.

Every 40 minutes, a Canadian woman dies of smoking-related causes.

Tobacco causes 80% of lung cancer, which is usually fatal. A heavy smoker is 18 times more likely to develop lung cancer than a non-smoker.

Smoking is a major cause of cancer of the throat, mouth, larynx, esophagus, pancreas, kidney and bladder.

In some regions of Canada and in every region of the United States lung cancer has already surpassed breast cancer as the major cancer killer of women.

Smokers are about three times more likely than non-smokers to develop cancer of the cervix. Women who don't smoke but are exposed to second-hand smoke are also much more likely to get cervical cancer.

"In my quitting ritual I will say good-bye to cigarettes.... I rid myself of dependence on a substance over which I have no control that has taken a good part of my life away. It has ruled and influenced all other choices I have made—has led to inertia of my body, my mind and my soul. I welcome control of my breath, of my life and my destiny. I yearn to be a child simply living, to be without chains, to decide and then do—to not simply think and smoke. I welcome activity of body and sparks in my mind and soul."

Smokers are more likely to develop all forms of cardiovascular disease, including strokes, thrombosis, hypertension and circulatory problems in the legs.

Women smoking half a pack a day double their chances of having a heart attack. Those smoking a pack and a half daily increase their likelihood of heart attack as much as tenfold.

Smoking while using birth control pills makes a woman twice as likely to have a heart attack. It increases the risk of stroke at least 30 times.

Smoking causes 82% of chronic obstructive lung diseases such as emphysema. These diseases are incapacitating.

A recent study has connected smoking to breast cancer.

Other Risks to Women Who Smoke

Women smokers experience more menstrual disorders, are less likely to conceive, and are 10 times more likely to miscarry.

Women smokers experience an earlier menopause and are more vulnerable to osteoporosis and periodontal disease.

Allergies and asthma are worsened by smoking.

Smokers are absent more often from work due to illness or injury.

Risks to Our Children

When a pregnant woman smokes she passes on carbon monoxide and nicotine to the baby, which decreases its supply of oxygen while at the same time increasing its heartbeat.

Smoking by parents or family members increases fetal and infant deaths.

A pregnant smoker has about twice the risk of a non-smoker of delivering a low birth-weight baby.

Nicotine can contaminate breast milk and be passed on to the baby.

Children of smokers are twice as likely to suffer from ailments such as ear infections, bronchitis and pneumonia. They are also more likely to become smokers themselves.

After reading this list you may wonder why tobacco companies are allowed to sell such a dangerous product. Many people around the world believe the promotion of cigarettes has gone on long enough and are trying to keep companies from doing more harm. If you want to learn more about these organizations, see the list of groups included at the back.

Even if you don't decide to join a group, it's still a good idea to express your anger and sense of injustice over the deaths and illnesses caused by the tobacco companies. Talk to friends and family and write about your feelings in your journal. Very often we forget that we are also victims of the tobacco industry.

It's a good idea to write these health facts on paper and place them around our homes to remind us of the truth about smoking.

Because smoking is such a powerful addiction, it is easy for us to shut out information about how it damages our health. The only way to heal the mind/body split is to pay attention to our bodies!

WHAT TO DO ON QUITTING DAY

1 Smoke your last cigarette and, if you wish, perform a ritual which honours your quitting.

2 Throw out all cigarettes. Get rid of lighters, matches and ashtrays.

3 Make sure you have lots of healthy snacks around, like carrot sticks, sunflower seeds and fruit.

4 Change your routine. Especially change the things you usually do when you smoke:
   - get up later
   - go to bed earlier
   - eat lunch standing up

5 Take lots of walks, short ones and long ones.

6 Drink lots of water. Avoid coffee, tea and alcohol.

7 Shower and bathe a couple of times.

8 Brush and floss your teeth often.

9 Chew sugarless gum.

10 Find things to do with your hands, such as writing, drawing, sewing, knitting, crossword puzzles or jigsaw puzzles. If you decide to write, do it in a place you don't associate with smoking.

11 Don't test yourself. Avoid smoking friends and smoking places. Spend time in non-smoking places such as the library.

12 Nap.

13 Call a friend. Talk about what you are going through.

14 Reward yourself by going out with non-smoking supportive friends or buying yourself a special treat.

15 Use your affirmations: *I am a non-smoker. I let go of my addiction.*

16 Remind yourself that your smoking urges only last a few minutes. They will pass with or without a cigarette. Do deep breathing through them. Imagine them as labour pains each one

"In my quitting ritual I would have to say 'Goodbye' to an old friend, who was there for me when I thought I needed him, but don't need or want him anymore. I'm okay now.... I'm strong and intelligent and not out of control of my life. I am in control and will quit for good—because I deserve it."

"My fears are not being able to stay away from cigarettes—justifying just one."

"No longer will my car smell stale. My clothes will be fresh. My hair and my body will be fresh. I will no longer have to look for a place to light up."

you get through brings you closer to birthing a new non-smoking you! Try timing your urges, so that you can see they actually do become shorter in duration and further apart.

17 Avoid difficult situations. If things get tough, let people know you've just quit smoking. Leave if necessary.

18 Experience your feelings. Write them down and talk about them.

19 Read over your reasons for quitting.

20 Read over the lists of the effects of smoking on the body.

You can do it!!!

WAYS TO COPE INSTEAD OF SMOKING

Each woman associates smoking with certain situations. You may want to turn back to Chapter 5 to review the times when you smoke. Preparing ourselves for the times when we know we will crave a cigarette can help us avoid smoking. Here are some triggers for smoking and alternative ways of coping with them.

Trigger	New Way to Cope
Talking on the phone	Keep the call brief. Tell your friend you can't talk very long because it makes it hard not to smoke. Doodle, deep breathe, walk around with the phone.
Completing a meal	Excuse yourself from the table. Let family or friends know this is a time you really miss smoking. Go for a walk. Brush your teeth. Deep breathe.

Trigger	New Way to Cope
Driving	Remove the ashtray and lighter from the car. Bring healthy treats you can eat in the car. Play music and sing along; say your affirmations out loud.
Conflict	If possible, remove yourself from the situation. Tell the person you're with that you've just quit smoking and this is a tough situation for you to be in without cigarettes. Use "I feel" statements and constructive criticism. Deep breathe. Remind yourself that smoking won't make it better. Think of all the negative aspects of smoking.
Bad news	Call a friend. Get support. Deep breathe. Express your feelings. Pray; meditate. Use affirmations and remind yourself that smoking won't make it better. Use positive self-talk. Get a massage.
Party or happy times	Plan ahead. Visualize yourself not smoking at the party. Plan what you will do instead. Remind yourself that smoking just one cigarette will hurt. Remember your reasons for quitting. Tell your friends how you're feeling.
Boredom	Shower, bathe, walk or read. Find something to do with your hands. Call a friend. Clean a drawer, closet, etc.

Trigger	New Way to Cope
Waking up or going to bed	Create a "self-care ritual." Spend more time brushing and flossing your teeth.
	Brush your hair.
	Do a short meditation or yoga practice.
	Drink water.
	Say a prayer.

One way of handling strong urges is to prevent them from happening. An acronym used by some stop-smoking groups to help ex-smokers avoid tough situations is *HALT*. This means don't get too:

Hungry
Angry
Lonely or
Tired (Delaney 1989).

The four Ds act as another reminder:

Delay
Deep Breathe
Drink Water
Do Something Else

QUITTING DATE

Choosing a day to quit smoking is a very significant act. It's a day worth marking forever. Any day you quit is a great day; here are some other dates that might help:

1 International Women's Day (March 8)
2 Earth Day (April 22)
3 Other special earth days—spring/fall equinox, winter/summer solstice
4 Important days in your life
5 Friday (This allows you a couple of days to experience withdrawal)

6 Birth date of someone who has inspired you (friend, author of important book)

7 The day after a challenging task or project is completed

8 The full moon or the new moon

RECOVERY/WITHDRAWAL/ HEALING SYMPTOMS

When you quit smoking your body will begin to recover from the effects of nicotine and the other chemicals found in cigarettes. Physical responses of withdrawal and recovery are just as diverse as emotional responses, so be prepared to accept a wide range of physical reactions. On the other hand, you may find that you experience very few recovery symptoms.

Recovery symptoms begin about one or two hours after your last cigarette and are most intense for the three days that follow quitting. It takes several months to flush the nicotine out of your entire system.

In Chapter 6 we touched on the concept of homeostasis. We said that part of our discomfort when we quit smoking is because of homeostasis—which is the body's way of keeping things stable. Homeostasis doesn't distinguish between "good" or "bad" changes. It resists all change and sends us signals that basically say, "Stop! What the heck are you trying to do—upset the balance I worked so hard to maintain?" (Leonard and Murphy 1995). It helps to understand homeostasis so that when things get tough we don't fool ourselves by thinking, "Gee, maybe I shouldn't quit; my body doesn't like it."

In fact, our bodies *do* want us to quit. Don't be alarmed by the discomfort you might feel. All of us have survived flus, colds, surgery or childbirth. If your body coped with smoking, it will have no

"So many things are happening around me lately. I'm trying to keep my children together as a family and I'm learning how to live in the empty nest."

"Just thinking about quitting has made me nervous."

"I will quit because I will feel better and have more energy and feel positive about my body and my health."

problem coping with not smoking. You can get through this!

The following list describes the most common recovery symptoms:

1 Coughing

Smoking paralyses the tiny hairs (cilia) in our lungs. When we quit, the cilia can return to their normal function and clear the tar out of our breathing passageways. Coughing is part of this process.

2 Slight Sore Throat

Our mouths and throats have been numbed by smoking. When we quit we can feel the damage smoking has done. Sometimes we will get a sore throat for a couple of days. Lozenges, cough syrup or a hot lemon and honey drink can help.

3 Headache or Dizziness

Research has shown that smokers metabolize caffeine differently from non-smokers. A smoker needs to drink more coffee than a non-smoker to get the same effect. As a result, if we don't lower our caffeine intake when we quit, we can suffer from headaches, dizziness or nervousness. We also get dizzy because we are adjusting to the increased flow of oxygen to our brains. Extra sleep, fresh air and massage can ease the discomfort of headaches.

4 Tiredness

Nicotine is a stimulant, so when we quit smoking we may find that we feel more tired than usual. An extra hour of sleep each night and exercise can help. In time, we will have more energy. *Tired All the Time: How to Regain Your Lost Energy* by Ronald Hoffman, M.D. is an excellent resource for learning more about the causes of fatigue.

5 Lack of Concentration

The "hit" of nicotine on our brains, plus the psychological association between smoking and work, often means we light up to focus on a task. When we quit it might seem as if we're not as alert. Try deep breathing. Avoid alcohol and caffeine.

6 Nervousness

When we quit we will be very sensitive to the nicotine remaining in our systems. This might make us feel on edge for a while. Drink lots of water, swim, walk and bathe to flush the nicotine out of your body.

7 Constipation or Diarrhoea

Smoking can alter the normal functioning of our bowels. When we quit we may experience some disturbances. Prunes, dried fruit or bran can get rid of constipation. Avoid caffeine to prevent diarrhoea.

8 Sleep Disturbances and Dreaming

It's very common to dream that we have been smoking or to be more aware of our dreams in general after we quit. The images and stories in our dreams can be fascinating. Sometimes they contain clues to why we smoke or how we might ease our recovery. Try writing down some of your dreams. We may also find we wake up earlier for the first few days after quitting. Our bodies are adjusting to the loss of nicotine. Deep breathing and doing relaxation exercises can help us achieve a more restful sleep.

9 Sugar Craving

Many ex-smokers experience strong cravings for sugar and sweets. Some researchers say it's because we can taste better. It has also been suggested that nicotine causes glucose that is stored in the liver to be released into the bloodstream. So when we quit, it takes a while for our bodies to adjust (Hoffman 1993). It's a good idea to keep lots of healthy foods handy so that we won't be tempted into swapping our cigarettes for a sugar addiction. Drinking lots of water and exercising can help.

Your Body Will Forgive You

One of the exciting aspects of quitting smoking is our bodies' capacity to heal from the damage. We can actually reduce the risk of acquiring smoking-related diseases to that of a non-smoker.

Don't ever think it's too late to quit smoking. Remember, your body will forgive you no matter how long you've been at it.

Thirty minutes after you quit: blood pressure, heart rate and temperature of hands and feet become normal.

Eight hours after you quit: carbon monoxide and oxygen levels in the blood return to normal.

Twenty-four hours after you quit: risks for heart attack and stroke decrease significantly.

Forty-eight hours after you quit: nerve endings in your mouth and nose regrow.

Seventy-two hours after you quit: bronchial tubes relax and breathing is easier.

One week after you quit: nicotine is flushed from your body.

Two weeks after you quit: circulation, breathing and lung function improve.

One month after you quit: coughing, sinus congestion and shortness of breath decrease.

Two years after you quit: risk of heart attack drops to that of a woman who has never smoked.

Five years after you quit: risk of stroke drops to normal; risk of lung cancer decreases by half.

Ten years after you quit: risk of most types of cancer drops to normal.

Fifteen years after you quit: risk of dying is similar to that of women who have never smoked!

Affirmations

Affirmations will be very useful in getting through strong urges and increasing your confidence.

It's important to create your own affirmations, but here are a few suggestions:

I am a non-smoker.
My body is strong and healthy.
I let go of my cigarettes with ease.
I am confident.
I am relaxed and calm.
I have chosen not to smoke.

Write these affirmations in your journal several times each day. As well, say them out loud and to yourself, especially when you get a strong urge to smoke.

Rewards

It's important to reward yourself for not smoking so you don't feel deprived and return to smoking as a way of nurturing yourself. Here are some suggestions—add your own to the list:

Daily Rewards

Bathe with candles and music

Have breakfast in bed

Buy a magazine

Weekly Rewards

Have lunch or supper out

Sleep in late

Read all morning

Go to a movie

Monthly Rewards

Buy a new outfit

Get a new hairstyle

Have a massage

Get a manicure

Get a tarot reading

Buy earrings

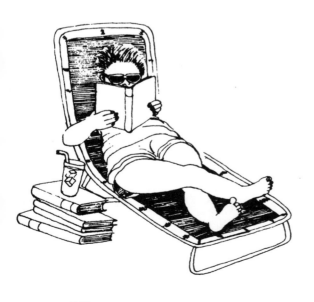

JOURNAL ENTRY: QUITTING

Prepare your space. Light a candle or burn incense.
Begin with the relaxation exercise or a few minutes of
conscious breathing. When you're ready, start writing.
Ask yourself:

What are my reasons for quitting?

What benefits will I see?

Describe a ritual or ceremony you can perform to say good-bye to smoking. An effective ritual is to write all your fears on a piece of paper and burn it. Another is to fill a bowl with salt water to represent the ocean and place your hands in the water, imagining all your fears and doubts flowing into the water.

At some point in your ceremony, acknowledge what smoking has meant to you. Then write or say out loud, "I can now let go of my cigarettes."

Imagine welcoming your new non-smoking self in some way. You could use an affirmation or the kind words you would choose to greet a long-lost friend.

Give yourself a reward when you are finished the exercise.

Obstacles to Staying Smoke-Free, and Relapse

Quitting smoking is always something to be proud of. Staying smoke-free is the goal of most quitters, but any attempt that keeps cigarettes out of our lives—even for just a few hours—helps us to become permanent non-smokers.

If we view quitting in this way we are more likely to keep our self-esteem intact if we have a slip or relapse. When we avoid "all-or-nothing" thinking, we help ourselves in two ways. First of all, our efforts to quit won't be totally ruined if we have one or two cigarettes. This doesn't mean that we should fool ourselves into believing we can smoke occasionally. It simply means if we do end up smoking a cigarette we should not abandon our attempt to quit. We can keep a slip from becoming a relapse by reminding ourselves of our reasons for quitting in the first place and recommitting ourselves to quitting.

The other way we can help ourselves avoid all-or-nothing thinking is to approach quitting one day (or even one moment) at a time. The thought of living without cigarettes for life may feel

"I get a strong urge to smoke only once in a while. I just tell myself, 'Forget it!' I know if I give in I'll be hooked again. I'm determined to stay quit. I want my body and mind back."

overwhelming. But if we break our lives down into individual days, then we can deal with each day as it arrives. We can say, "I will do what I need to move through *this* day without smoking!"

The urge to smoke is usually incredibly strong during the first few days after we quit, but after a couple of weeks (sooner for some women) you will find yourself not thinking about smoking for a few days at a time. Eventually you will go for weeks without thinking about smoking!

Staying smoke-free also means putting ourselves first. We need to practise mindfulness and check-ins to keep in touch with how we're feeling and what we need to do, so we don't fall back on cigarettes. We also need to talk to our families and friends about how they can help. Using "I feel" statements and constructive criticism is a useful technique to let people know when they are not being helpful.

It's a good idea to be as specific as possible when asking for support. Ask for a back rub, tea, a night out, help with your kids or whatever you need to make the transition from smoker to non-smoker. It's also a good idea to make agreements with people in advance, so that you don't find yourself having a bad day with no help in sight. You could have one friend agree to babysit for you one evening each week for the first month, another friend call you every evening for the first week and another friend give you a massage. When we spread our requests for support among friends, we're not as likely to feel guilty for asking for too much from one friend. We also decrease the risk of being left with no support at all.

"I started smoking again after I had my baby. I guess I would have to say I felt happy because it marked a return to the 'old' self."

During the days and weeks between quitting and feeling strong in our non-smoking status we need to surround ourselves with people who want us to succeed. Although many people might have encouraged us to quit smoking, we may be surprised to discover that some of them are unable to help us stay off cigarettes. Every now and then we may encounter friends or family members who actually try to sabotage our efforts to become non-smokers. There are lots of reasons behind this.

One of the reasons is that quitting smoking can threaten those who still smoke. If we find our smoking friends becoming defensive, we need to be clear that we have quit for us, not to impress others or to feel superior. Just as we needed respect and patience, so do our friends who still smoke.

If our partners smoke we will need to be especially honest and open about our feelings. It's a good idea to agree on some rules about when and where they can smoke so that we are not being continually tempted and tested.

Our friends and families may not be prepared for the consequences that our quitting smoking will have for them. Since it may be necessary for us to avoid places where there is smoking, we may sometimes have to avoid them. (Social situations are one of the highest-rated relapse situations.) Not surprisingly, a few of them would be happier if we would light up again. It's not that they want to see us fail; they just really miss having us around. It's important to talk about our feelings and actively pursue new ways of being together with our friends.

Spending time alone will be just as important as being with others. A part of each of our days should be spent quietly, so that we have time to relax and reflect on our reasons for wanting to live smoke-free. Writing, reading, walking or listening to music should become part of our daily routine. These quiet times can provide us with valuable insights into who we are and what we need to feel well—emotionally and physically.

Remember, smoking a cigarette is in some ways like "taking a pill" to solve our problems. Although smoking might appear to help us, in the same way certain medications appear to help us, it really

"I passed through the physical withdrawal symptoms after a couple of days. It was very difficult to disassociate smoking from doing just about anything. I experienced a lack of concentration and I wanted to cry, complain and bitch. I realized I must avoid lethargic activities—just sitting around and talking. I needed to constantly remind myself that cigarettes have been the master for a quarter of a century! I can never let myself believe there could be just one cigarette."

doesn't. There are no quick fixes to getting well. Quitting smoking is the equivalent of trading a "pill-popping" approach to life for a natural, less dramatic way of coping. Quitting smoking involves us "sobering up" to the fact that what we turn to for comfort is actually killing us. This is often a painful realization. It's a process of losing faith, similar to discovering that a trusted friend has been lying to us or that a relationship we desperately want to maintain simply has too many destructive aspects to make it workable.

We can draw strength from the experiences of other women who have survived quitting and are happier for having done it. Their stories can bolster our faith that we, too, will find something even better than smoking.

LIVING SMOKE-FREE

"It took me a few times to quit for good. But I know I've quit for good this time and it feels wonderful."

Eventually life without cigarettes will feel normal. We will no longer watch the clock or count the days since we quit smoking. We will feel proud of ourselves for leaving behind a serious addiction. But until not smoking feels like second nature, it's important to avoid certain situations that can get us hooked again.

1   Remember that the urge to smoke will pass.
Try deep breathing, stretching or any of the other coping techniques discussed in Chapter 10.

2   Plan what you will do in difficult situations.
The American Lung Association suggests you cope
with strong urges in the following ways:
- wait it out
- change your routine
- change your thinking
- escape

3   Let people know what you need. Be specific.
Remember that it's okay to put yourself first. You are
not bad or selfish for asking for what you want.

4   Avoid alcohol.
Drinking alcohol can weaken our resolve and give us
a false sense of confidence. We might start thinking
we can smoke just this once.

5   Sleep well and eat well.
Smokers often use cigarettes when we should rest or
eat. Regular meals and healthy snacks can keep us
from reaching for cigarettes. Also, feeling hungry
and tired can worsen our emotional state and
increase our anxiety.

6   Walk, swim, jump, run, stretch.
Daily exercise can keep us from gaining unwanted
weight and can increase our emotional and physical
stamina.

7   Remember to reward yourself.
If you smoked a pack a day, after one week of not
smoking you have saved yourself about $35 to $56.
Spend this money on you!

JOURNAL ENTRY: STAYING SMOKE-FREE

Prepare your space. Light a candle or burn incense. Start with the relaxation exercise or a few minutes of conscious breathing. When you're ready, begin writing. Ask yourself:

What has been the toughest part about not smoking?

What difficult situation did I already get through?

What will help me stay smoke-free?

When you are finished reward yourself.

Who Are We Now?

We never really know how much of our lives revolves around smoking until we quit. Suddenly pockets of time appear during the day, and we are not quite sure what to do with them. We no longer scramble for those extra minutes in the morning to have a cigarette. We can take our breaks when we want—instead of when a smoking urge demands it. And we don't have to rush through our activities to get to the cigarette at the end. Life has a different rhythm now, because we no longer structure our time around when and where we can smoke.

Changing how we spend time is profound. It affects everything about us. That's why quitting smoking is more than just stopping a bad habit. As we discussed in Chapter 6, quitting smoking means changing our way of being in the world. How we conduct our intimate relationships with friends, our children and our partners, how we work and how we spend our leisure time all change when we become non-smokers. We change our identity.

Some changes in identity are thrust upon us

"I would like to take time to recognize my personal needs—to take time to slow down; not fill every evening on my calendar."

without our consent or desire. Quitting smoking is an identity change that we initiate. We recognize that the old us (in this case the smoker) is no longer who we want to be. This doesn't mean that we have to feel badly or ashamed of who we were. We can acknowledge that smoking served a purpose in our lives, and at the same time acknowledge that it hurt us. Both types of identity changes, the ones we invite and the ones that happen unexpectedly, involve some sense of loss and distress—no matter how positive they may turn out to be.

Quitting smoking means saying good-bye to the self that believed "smoking makes it better" and welcoming the new self who enjoys life without cigarettes.

When we give up the ways we related to the world as smokers, we won't immediately know what to do with ourselves. Perhaps we will feel slightly panicky and anxious while we wait for the new self to arrive. Without our cigarettes the days might seem long and empty at first. But if we think of quitting smoking as part of a healthy change in identity, we can view the empty places in our lives as places full of potential.

William Bridges (1980), in his book *Transitions*, describes the place between an ending and a new beginning as the neutral zone. The neutral zone is "a seemingly unproductive time when we feel disconnected from people and things in the past and emotionally unconnected to the present." He believes that the neutral zone experience is the natural result of the ending process and that we must give in to the emptiness. He sees this time as a very necessary and important (although unpleasant) part of change.

Barbara Sher (1994), another author who writes about the challenges of changing, says,

> Most of the rewarding things in life—riding a bicycle, traveling in a foreign country, or making love—begin with incompetence and embarrassment. What will determine the course of your life more than any one thing is whether or not you are willing to tolerate necessary discomfort.

There are several ways to make the neutral zone experience easier on ourselves. Some of the ways already suggested, such as spending time alone, writing our thoughts and feelings down and practising affirmations, are very useful. Bridges also suggests writing an autobiography, thinking about what would be unlived in our lives if they ended today, and taking a few days to go on our own version of a rite-of-passage journey.

The idea of a rite-of-passage journey could be especially meaningful to us as ex-smokers. A ceremony to mark our identity change could also help us celebrate restoring the health we compromised when we began smoking.

"I can relate to the 'dead space' in my life when changes are happening. What do we do when we sit through anxious moments, or feel overwhelmed by conflict, strung out with stress? We normally console ourselves with a cigarette."

"A rite of passage? Yes! I believe it should be an event that takes place over a period of two to three days. I would choose to join kindred spirits in a lovely secluded setting surrounded by nature, huge trees, a running stream or lake, rocks, mountains, fresh air, silence of nature, places to walk that were safe, time to reflect, read and participate in discussion on your reflections. A chance for renewal in the deepest sense. Rebirth."

Quitting smoking can awaken a deep craving for life within us and can give us the confidence to make other changes that we thought were impossible. We may find ourselves thinking about returning to school, changing jobs or moving. All of these changes can be made in time. What's important to remember is that we need to take special care of ourselves during this transition and not take on too many new changes at once.

Our reasons for quitting and our attitude toward change will affect how easy or difficult we find the transition. If we cling to the old belief that smoking can enrich our lives, we will see quitting as an act of self-deprivation. But if we are committed to seeing quitting as an act of self-renewal we can move through the tough times and the uncertain times with more faith and determination.

"To take a rite of passage I would be at home with two or preferably three days away from my job or any other responsibilities. I would sleep and nap as much as possible. I would not talk on the phone. I would snack on fresh fruits. I would take a long walk to the park. I would perhaps see a movie by myself or visit a non-smoking friend, briefly. I would watch the birds, look at the flowers. I would remind myself that I am in control of my life and that I choose not to smoke."

JOURNAL ENTRY: WHO ARE WE NOW?

Prepare your space. Light a candle or burn incense. Start with the relaxation exercise or a few minutes of conscious breathing. When you are ready, begin writing. Ask yourself:

What empty places have I discovered in my life?

Knowing that you can take whatever time you need to change, describe some of the things you would like to change about your life.

Describe a three- or four-day rite-of-passage journey you could take to acknowledge your identity change from smoker to non-smoker. For example, would you camp and fast for three days or treat yourself to a night or two alone in a hotel? What would you do? Where would it happen?

When you are finished, reward yourself.

Staying on Our Path

Addictions keep us in a constant state of inner conflict. Most of us who are addicted to cigarettes want to experience a high level of health and well-being. Instead, we end up compromising much of what we believe is important—our health, our families' health and our environment. Our addictions limit our ability to live in accordance with our values. They exact a price.

It takes a lot of determination and honesty to come to terms with the price we pay for smoking and then quit. When we do quit we reclaim and reconnect with a source of inner strength that was always inside of us. This is no small discovery. Learning to listen to ourselves and believe in our own wisdom takes practice and hard work. It is the key to living a self-directed life.

The shift from smoker to non-smoker is meaningful in many different ways. It might be the first time we take control over our lives. It might be the first action in clearing our lives of other unhealthy behaviours. It may be a touchstone of strength—the

one thing we can point to in times of chaos and self-doubt and say, *"I never thought I could quit smoking, but I did. I can make other changes too!"*

The path to quitting is really the path home to our true selves. It's a journey that will serve us well in life, long after we have forgotten about our cigarettes. As with many journeys, we might stop and start a few times, lose sight of our destination and doubt our strength to go the distance. But if we take one step at a time we will get there. May you trust in your ability to make the trip and may you dance at least part of the way!

Notes:

Notes:

Notes:

Notes:

References

Adair, Margo. 1984. *Working Inside Out: Tools for Change*. Berkeley: Wingbow Press.

American Lung Association. 1984. *Freedom from Smoking: Guide for Clinic Leaders*. Revised Edition. New York: American Lung Association.

American Lung Association. 1986. *Freedom from Smoking in 20 Days: Self-Help Quit Smoking Program*. New York: American Lung Association.

American Lung Association. 1986. *A Lifetime of Freedom from Smoking*. New York: American Lung Association.

Baar, Karen. 1994. "The Real Options in Healthcare." *Natural Health Magazine* (November/December).

Bovey, Shelley. 1989. *Being Fat Is Not a Sin*. London: Pandora Press.

Bridges, William. 1980. *Transitions: Making Sense of Life's Changes*. Menlo Park: Addison-Wesley.

British Columbia, Provincial Health Officer. 1996. *A report on the health of British Columbians: Provincial Health Officer's Annual Report 1995*. Victoria, B.C.: Ministry of Health and Ministry Responsible for Seniors.

Canadian Council on Smoking and Health. 1989. *Taking Control: An Action Handbook on Women and Tobacco*. Ottawa: Canadian Council on Smoking and Health.

Capacchione, Lucia. 1989. *The Well-Being Journal: Drawing on your inner power to heal yourself*. North Hollywood: Newcastle Publishing Co., Inc.

Chopra, Deepak. 1987. *Creating Health: Beyond Prevention, Toward Perfection*. Boston: Houghton Mifflin Company.

References

Clark, Lisa, and Lisa Shaw-Verhoek. August 1988. *Dying for a Smoke: Why Some Women Go That Far!* Independent Inquiry Project, Master of Social Work, School of Social Work, Carleton University, Ottawa.

Cobb, Janine O'Leary. 1988. "Women and Cigarettes." *A Friend Indeed: for women in the prime of life* 5, no. 7 (December).

Cooper, Robert K. 1989. *Health & Fitness Excellence: The Scientific Action Plan*. Boston: Houghton Mifflin Company.

Cunningham, Donna, and Andrew Ramer. 1988. *The Spiritual Dimensions of Healing Addictions*. San Rafael: Cassandra Press.

Cunningham, Donna, and Andrew Ramer. 1989. *Further Dimensions of Healing Addictions*. San Rafael: Cassandra Press.

Delaney, Sue S. 1989. *Women Smokers Can Quit: A Different Approach*. Evanston: Women's Healthcare Press.

Fields, Rick, et al. 1984. *Chop Wood, Carry Water: A Guide to Finding Spiritual Fulfillment in Everyday Life*. New York: Jeremy P. Tarcher, Inc.

Forbes, W.F., R.C. Frecker, and D. Nostbakken, eds. 1983. *Proceedings of the Fifth World Conference on Smoking and Health* (Winnipeg). Ottawa: Canadian Council on Smoking and Health.

Gershon, David, and Gail Straub. 1989. *Empowerment: The Art of Creating Your Life As You Want It*. New York: Dell Publishing.

Goldberg, Natalie. 1986. *Writing Down the Bones: Freeing the Writer Within*. Boston: Shambhala Publications, Inc.

Greaves, Lorraine, for Health and Welfare Canada. 1987. Background Paper on Women and Tobacco. Ottawa: Health and Welfare Canada.

———, for the Women and Tobacco Reduction Program, Health Canada. 1995. *Mixed Messages: Women, Tobacco and the Media, Canada, 1989-1994*. Ottawa: Health Canada.

———. 1996. *Smoke Screen: Women's Smoking and Social Control*. Halifax: Fernwood Publishing.

Hagan, Kay Leigh. 1988. *Internal Affairs: A Journalkeeping Workbook for Self-Intimacy*. Atlanta: Escapadia Press.

Hanh, Thich Nhat. 1991. *Peace Is Every Step: The Path of Mindfulness in Everyday Life*. New York: Bantam Books.

Health and Welfare Canada. March 1988. *National Workshop on Women and Tobacco Proceedings*.

Health and Welfare Canada. August 1994. *Survey on Smoking in Canada, Cycle 1: Profile of Women*.

Health Canada. 1995. *Tobacco Use among High Priority Groups: Fact Sheets.*

Hoffman, Ronald L. 1993. *Tired All the Time: How to Regain Your Lost Energy.* New York: Simon and Schuster.

Horne, Tammy. April 1995. *Women and Tobacco: A Framework for Action.* Ottawa: Health Canada.

Hutchinson, Marcia Germaine. 1985. *Transforming Body Image: Learning to Love the Body You Have.* Trumansburg: The Crossing Press.

Jacobson, Bobbie. 1986. *Beating the Ladykillers: Women and Smoking.* London: Pluto Press.

Kabat-Zinn, Jon. 1990. *Full Catastrophe Living: Using the Wisdom of Your Body and Mind to Face Stress, Pain, and Illness.* New York: Dell Publishing.

Kano, Susan. 1985. *Making Peace with Food: Freeing Yourself from the Diet/Weight Obsession.* Danbury, Conn.: Amity Publishing Company.

Krogh, David. 1991. *Smoking: The Artificial Passion.* Oxford: W.H. Freeman and Company.

Leonard, George, and Michael Murphy. 1995. *The Life We Are Given: A Long-Term Program for Realizing the Potential of Body, Mind, Heart, and Soul.* New York: G.P. Putnam's Sons.

Levine, Stephen. 1979. *A Gradual Awakening.* Garden City: Anchor Books.

Louden, Jennifer. 1992. *The Woman's Comfort Book: A Self-Nurturing Guide for Restoring Balance in Your Life.* San Francisco: Harper Collins.

Mariechild, Diane. 1981. *Mother Wit: A Feminist Guide to Psychic Development.* Trumansburg: The Crossing Press.

Marsh, Alan. 1984. "Smoking: Habit or Choice." *Population Trends* 37, no. 20.

Murphy, Michael. 1992. *The Future of the Body: Explorations into the Further Evolution of Human Nature.* New York: G.P. Putnam's Sons.

Peele, Stanton, Archie Brodsky, with Mary Arnold. 1991. *The Truth about Addiction and Recovery: The Life Process Program for Outgrowing Destructive Habits.* New York: Simon and Schuster.

Persaud, Vena, Betty-Anne Pawliw-Fry, and Susan Jackson. 1995. *Priority Women and Tobacco Project: Assessment of Existing Smoking Cessation Programs for Priority Women, April 1995.*

Prochaska, James O., John C. Norcross, and Carlo C. DiClemente. 1994. *Changing for Good: The Revolutionary Program That Explains the Six Stages of Change and Teaches You How to Free Yourself from Bad Habits*. New York: William Morrow and Company.

Reading, Jeff, for Health Canada. 1996. *Eating Smoke: A Literature Review of the Non-Traditional Use of Tobacco among Aboriginal People*. Ottawa: Ministry of Supply and Social Services.

Roth, Gabrielle, with John Loudon. 1989. *Maps to Ecstasy: teachings of an urban shaman*. San Rafael: New World Library.

Sandmaier, Marian. 1984. "Alcohol, Mood-Altering Drugs and Smoking." In *The New Our Bodies, Ourselves: A Book by and for Women*, edited by The Boston Women's Health Book Collective. New York: Simon and Schuster.

Schwartz, Jerome L. April 1987. *Review and Evaluation of Smoking Cessation Methods: The United States and Canada, 1978-1985*. Bethesda, Maryland: National Institutes of Health.

Schwartz, Tony. 1995. *What Really Matters: Searching for Wisdom in America*. New York: Bantam Books.

Sher, Barbara, with Barbara Smith. 1994. *I Could Do Anything If I Only Knew What It Was: How to Discover What You Really Want and How to Get It*. New York: Dell Publishing Group, Inc.

Spangler, Tina. 1994. "Is Your Bedroom Making You Sick?" *Natural Health Magazine* (June).

Travis, John, and Regina Sara Ryan. 1987. *The Wellness Workbook*. Berkeley: Ten Speed Press.

———. 1991. *Wellness: Small Changes You Can Use to Make a Big Difference*. Berkley: Ten Speed Press.

Tschirhart Sanford, Linda, and Mary Ellen Donovan. 1984. *Women and Self-Esteem: Understanding and Improving the Way We Think and Feel about Ourselves*. New York: Penguin.

Wolinsky, Stephen, with Margaret O. Ryan. 1991. *Trances People Live: Healing Approaches in Quantum Psychology*. Connecticut: The Bramble Company.

World Health Organization, Tobacco or Health Programme. 31 May 1989. *The Female Smoker: At Added Risk, World's 2nd No-Tobacco Day*. Fact Sheet.

Further Reading

The following list includes just a few selections from the hundreds of excellent books available on these subjects. Most of these books can be found at your local library.

Addictions
The Truth about Addiction and Recovery by Stanton Peele and Archie Brodsky with Mary Arnold. Simon and Schuster, 1991.

Body
Being Fat Is Not a Sin by Shelley Bovey. Pandora Press, 1989.

Breaking All the Rules: Feeling Good and Looking Great, No Matter What Your Size by Nancy Roberts. Penguin, 1987.

The Life We Are Given: A Long-Term Program for Realizing the Potential of Body, Mind, Heart, and Soul by George Leonard and Michael Murphy. G.P. Putnam's Sons, 1995.

Living Binge Free: A Personal Guide to Victory over Compulsive Eating by James Evan Latimer. Living Quest, 1988.

Making Peace with Food: Freeing Yourself from the Diet/Weight Obsession by Susan Kano. Amity Publishing Company, 1985.

Mastery: The Keys to Success and Long-Term Fulfillment by George Leonard. Penguin, 1992.

Transforming Body Image: Learning to Love the Body You Have by Marcia Germaine Hutchinson. The Crossing Press, 1985.

Women's Experience of Sex: The Facts and Feelings of Female Sexuality at Every Stage of Life by Sheila Kitzinger. Penguin, 1985.

Change
Changing for Good: The Revolutionary Program That Explains the Six Stages of Change and Teaches You How to Free Yourself from Bad

Habits by James Prochaska, John Norcross and Carlo DiClemente.
William Morrow and Co., Inc., 1994.

*Chop Wood, Carry Water: A Guide to Finding Spiritual Fulfillment in
Everyday Life* by Rick Fields with Peggy Taylor, Rex Weyler, and Rick
Ingrasci. Jeremy P. Tarcher, Inc., 1984.

*The Dance of Anger: A Woman's Guide to Changing the Patterns of Intimate
Relationships* by Harriet Goldhor Lerner. Perennial Library, 1985.

Postpartum Depression and Anxiety: A Self-Help Guide for Mothers by
Pacific Postpartum Support Society, 1987.

*The Seven Habits of Highly Effective People: Powerful Lessons in Personal
Change* by Stephen Covey. A Fireside Book, 1990.

The Six Pillars of Self-Esteem by Nathaniel Branden. Bantam, 1984.

Transitions: Making Sense of Life's Changes by William Bridges. Addison-
Wesley, 1980.

*Women and Self-Esteem: Understanding and Improving the Way We
Think and Feel about Ourselves* by Linda Tschirhart Sanford and
Mary Ellen Donovan. Penguin, 1984.

Working Inside Out: Tools for Change by Margo Adair. Wingbow Press,
1984.

Food

Diet for a Small Planet by Francis Moore Lappe. Ballantine, 1982.

*Eat More, Weigh Less: Dr. Dean Ornish's Life Choice Program for Losing
Weight Safely While Eating Abundantly* by Dean Ornish, M.D.
Harper. Perennial, 1994.

*Fast Vegetarian Feasts: Delicious Healthy Meals You Can Make in
Forty-five Minutes or Less* by Martha Rose Shulman. Doubleday,
1986.

The Moosewood Cookbook and *The Enchanted Broccoli Forest* by Mollie
Katzen. Ten Speed Press, 1982.

The Tao of Cooking by Sally Pasley. Ten Speed Press, 1982.

Healing

The Courage to Heal: A Guide for Women Survivors of Child Sexual Abuse
by Ellen Bass and Laura Davis. Perennial Library, 1988.

Getting Free: A Handbook for Women in Abusive Relationships by Ginny
NiCarthy. The Seal Press, 1987.

The Ones Who Got Away: Women Who Left Abusive Partners by Ginny
NiCarthy. The Seal Press, 1987.

Trances People Live: Healing Approaches in Quantum Psychology by Stephen Wolinsky with Margaret O. Ryan. Bramble Co., 1991.

Trauma and Recovery by Judith Lewis Herman, M.D.. Harper Collins, 1992.

Health

Ageless Body, Timeless Mind: The Quantum Alternative to Growing Old by Deepak Chopra. Harmony Books, 1993.

Health & Fitness Excellence: The Scientific Action Plan by Robert K. Cooper. Addison-Wesley, 1989.

The New Our Bodies, Ourselves: A Book by and for Women by The Boston Women's Health Book Collective. Simon and Schuster, 1984.

Ourselves Growing Older by Paula Brown Doress and Diana Laskin Siegal and The Midlife and Older Women Book Project. Simon and Schuster, 1987.

Self-Help For Premenstrual Syndrome: A New and Expanded Edition by Michelle Harrison. Random House, 1985.

The Wellness Workbook by John W. Travis and Regina Sara Ryan. Ten Speed Press, 1987.

Massage

The Massage Book by George Downing. Random House/Bookworks, 1972.

The Sensual Body by Lucy Lidell. Gaia Books Ltd., 1987.

The Therapeutic Touch: How to Use Your Hands to Help or Heal by Delores Kreiger. Prentice-Hall, 1979.

Meditation

Full Catastrophe Living: Using the Wisdom of Your Body and Mind to Face Stress, Pain and Illness by Jon Kabat-Zinn. Dell Publishing, 1990.

A Path with Heart: A Guide Through the Perils and Promises of Spiritual Life by Jack Kornfield. Bantam, 1993.

Peace Is Every Step: The Path of Mindfulness in Everyday Life by Thich Nhat Hanh. Bantam, 1991.

Money and Work

I Could Do Anything If I Only Knew What It Was: How to Discover What You Really Want and How to Get It by Barbara Sher and Barbara Smith. Dell, 1994.

Mindfulness and Meaningful Work: Explorations in Right Livelihood,
edited by Claude Whitmyer. Parallax Press, 1994.
*Your Money or Your Life: Transforming Your Relationship with Money and
Achieving Financial Independence* by Joe Dominguez and Vicki
Robin. Penguin, 1992.

Movement
*Awareness Through Movement: Easy-to-Do Health Exercises to Improve
Your Posture, Vision, Imagination, and Personal Awareness* by Moshe
Feldenkrais. Harper and Row, 1972.

Self-Care
*The Woman's Comfort Book: A Self-Nurturing Guide for Restoring
Balance in Your Life* by Jennifer Louden. Harper Collins, 1992.

Smoking
Act Now: Women and Tobacco by The Working Group on Women and
Tobacco. National Strategy to Reduce Tobacco Use, Health and
Welfare Canada, 1994.
Beating the Ladykillers: Women and Smoking by Bobbie Jacobson. Pluto
Press, 1986.
Smoke Screen: Women's Smoking and Social Control by Lorraine Greaves.
Fernwood Publishing, 1996.
Taking Control: An Action Handbook on Women and Tobacco by Lorraine
Greaves. Canadian Council on Smoking and Health, 1989.
Women Smokers Can Quit: A Different Approach by Sue Delaney.
Women's Healthcare Press, 1989.

Writing
If You Want to Write: A Book about Art, Independence and Spirit by
Brenda Euland. Graywolf Press, 1987.
Internal Affairs: A Journalkeeping Workbook for Self-Intimacy by Kay
Leigh Hagan. Escapadia Press, 1988.
*The New Diary: How to use a journal for self guidance and expanded cre-
ativity* by Tristine Rainer. St. Martin's Press, 1978.
Wild Mind: Living the Writer's Life by Natalie Goldberg. Bantam, 1990.
Writing Down the Bones: Freeing the Writer Within by Natalie Goldberg.
Shambhala Publications, Inc., 1986.

Organizations

Aboriginal Women in the Canadian Labour Force
34-283 Bannatyne Avenue
Winnipeg, MB
R3B 3B2

Action on Women's Addictions - Research and Education (AWARE)
P.O. Box 86
Kingston, ON
K7L 4V6
Phone: (613) 545-0117 Fax: (613) 545-1508

Addiction Research Foundation
33 Russell Street
Toronto, ON
M5S 2S1
Phone: (416) 595-6889 Fax: (416) 595-6899

Canadian Association for the Advancement of Women and Sport and Physical Activity (CAAWS)
1600 James Naismith Drive
Gloucester, ON
K1B 5N4
Phone: (613) 748-5793 Fax: (613) 748-5775

Canadian Cancer Society
10 Elkhorn Avenue, Suite 200
Toronto, ON
M4V 3B1
Phone: (416) 961-7223 Fax: (416) 961-4189

Canadian Council on Smoking and Health

1000-170 Laurier Avenue West
Ottawa, ON
K1P 5V5
Phone: (613) 567-3050 Fax: (613) 567-2730

Canadian Network on Women and Tobacco (CANWAT)

c/o Canadian Council on Smoking and Health (see above)

Canadian Public Health Association

1565 Carling Avenue, Suite 400
Ottawa, ON
K1Z 8R1

Canadian Research Institute for the Advancement of Women

151 Slater Street, Suite 408
Ottawa, ON
K1P 5H3
Phone: (613) 563-0681 Fax: (613) 563-0682

Canadian Women's Health Network

c/o Women's Health Clinic
419 Graham Avenue, 3rd Floor
Winnipeg, MB
R3C 0M3
Phone: (204) 947-2422, ext. 134 Fax: (204) 943-3844

Health Canada Women and Tobacco Reduction Programs
Health Promotion Directorate

Jeanne Mance Building, Tunney's Pasture
Ottawa, ON
K1A 1B4
Phone: (613) 957-8335 Fax: (613) 952-5188

Heart and Stroke Foundation of Canada

160 George Street, Suite 200
Ottawa, ON
K1N 9M2
Phone: (613) 241-4361 Fax: (613) 241-3278

International Network of Women Against Tobacco (INWAT)
American Public Health Association
1015 Fifteenth Street N.W., Suite 300
Washington, D.C. 20005
Phone: (202) 789-5689 Fax: (202) 789-5661

The Lung Association
1900 City Park Drive, Suite 508
Blair Business Park
Gloucester ON
K1J 1A3
Phone: (613) 747-6776 Fax: (613) 747-7430

National Action Committee on the Status of Women
Suite 203, 234 Eglington Avenue
Toronto, ON
M4P 1K5
Phone: (416) 932-1718 Fax: (416) 932-0646

National Anti-Poverty Organization
256 King Edward Avenue
Ottawa, ON
K1N 7M1
Phone: (613) 789-0096 Fax: (613) 789-0141

National Clearing House on Tobacco and Health
1000-170 Laurier Avenue West
Ottawa, ON
K1P 5V5
Phone: 1-800-267-5234 or (613) 567-3050 Fax: (613) 567-5695

National Watch on Images of Women in the Media Inc.
517 Wellingon Street West, Suite 204
Toronto, ON
M5V 1G1
Phone: (416) 408-2065 Fax: (416) 408-2069

Native Women's Association of Canada
9 Melrose Avenue
Ottawa, ON
K1Y 1T8

Physicians for a Smoke-Free Canada
1000-170 Laurier Avenue West
Ottawa, ON
K1P 5V5
Phone: (613) 233-4878 Fax: (613) 567-2730

The Traditional Native American Seed Bank and Education Program (TNAT)
c/o Joseph Winter and Lawrence Shorty
Department of Anthropology
University of New Mexico
Albuquerque, NM 87131

Women and Tobacco Reduction Programs -Health Promotion Directorate - Health Canada
Jeanne Mance Building, Tunney's Pasture
Ottawa, ON
K1A 1B4
Phone: (613) 957-8335 Fax: (613) 952-5188

World Health Organization - Distribution and Sales
1211 Geneva 27
Switzerland

About Women's Health Clinic

Started in 1981, Women's Health Clinic is a feminist, community-based health centre, offering a range of services to women from teens to elders. Our holistic approach emphasizes prevention, education and action. We encourage women to learn all they can about what contributes to their health and well-being so they can make informed choices. We serve as the Manitoba base for the Canadian Women's Health Network.

Health Services

A multi-disciplinary team composed of physicians, a nurse practitioner, a nutritionist, counsellors and client service workers provides individual care for:

- Pregnancy Testing
- Unplanned Pregnancy
- Birth Control
- Sexually Transmitted Diseases

- AIDS Testing and Counselling
- Premenstrual Syndrome
- Menopause
- Weight Preoccupation
- Teen Clinic

Support Groups and Special Programs

We offer support groups for women to share information and emotional support around particular women's health issues such as weight preoccupation/body image, midlife and wellness, and breast implants.

Community Education

We offer speakers on women's health issues for community and professional groups and information sessions on health topics of concern to women, e.g., smoking, menopause, endometriosis, midwifery.

Volunteer Opportunities

We train volunteers to provide:
- Individual peer counselling to women about birth control, unplanned pregnancy, postpartum adjustment and weight preoccupation.
- Speaking engagements in the community on women's health issues.

About the Author

Deborah Holmberg-Schwartz has worked as a counsellor, managing editor of *Herizons Magazine*, women's centre coordinator, life skills instructor and group facilitator. She is an activist on women's health issues and wrote the first edition of *Catching Our Breath* and *Guide for Facilitators*. She currently lives in Nelson, British Columbia, with her husband and four children, where she facilitates Catching Our Breath groups and works as a private consultant.

Deborah Holmberg-Schwartz welcomes your comments about *Catching Our Breath* as well as your stories about smoking and quitting. She can be reached through Women's Health Clinic in Winnipeg or at her home:

R.R.#1, S-7, C-7
South Slocan, B.C.
V0G 2G0
e-mail: Deborah@netidea.com

For information about ordering more copies of this book or
the companion facilitator's guide, contact:
Women's Health Clinic
3rd floor – 419 Graham Avenue
Winnipeg, Manitoba
R3C 0M3 Canada
Telephone: (204) 947-1517 TTY: (204) 956-0385 Fax: (204) 943-3844.